Dear
Enjoy ve
a grain of

MW01236352

SCENES BEYOND THE GRAVE

VISIONS
of
MARIETTA DAVIS

Edited by Gordon Lindsay

Thirty-Sixth Edition

Published by
CHRIST FOR THE NATIONS, INC.
Dallas, TX 75224
Reprint 2002

STATEMENT BY
PUBLISHER OF THE NEW EDITION

So great was the interest in the original publication of the book, SCENES BEYOND THE GRAVE, which appeared in print approximately a century ago, that no less than twenty-three editions followed within a period of a few years. One hundred years have elapsed since that time and most of the books of that day have been forgotten and have lost their value, except as historical records. But in the case of SCENES BEYOND THE GRAVE, we consider it a most unfortunate omission that no publisher of recent time so far as we know has made available to the present generation, so important a document. (Portions of the narrative appeared in tract form some years ago.)

Though the present edition, which we now present, has been slightly abridged, it is believed that no important part of Marietta's remarkable narrative has been omitted. Here and there an obsolete word or phrase, a paragraph containing repetition, descriptive material not altogether essential to the story, has been deleted. This limited amount of editing we believe has increased the readability and value of the book to the average person. We would emphasize that nothing has been added—the story as it appears is entirely the words of Marietta Davis, as recorded by her pastor, Rev. J. L. Scott.

Although many witnesses attest the genuineness of the experiences of Marietta, nothing speaks more of the book's authenticity than the contents themselves. Doctrinally its message agrees absolutely with the Scriptural revelation as to the character of man's existence after death. The story gives many additional details, which depict clearly what takes place when the human spirit leaves the body. Needless to say the unfolding drama is

2

a most solemn object lesson, to which each reader will do well to take heed.

Further comment on the narrative is unnecessary, though not a few points are of significance which are worthy of special notice. Marietta lived at a time when the Church took little or no notice of the truth so emphasized in the New Testament—the Second Coming of Christ. It is therefore noteworthy to observe the angel's words spoken to Marietta on one occasion which clearly indicated that relatively the time of that event was approaching even then: "Man's redemption draweth nigh. Let angels swell the chorus; for soon the Saviour descendeth with holy attending angels." We cannot forebear to observe also the Great Commission as given by the Lord Jesus Christ in Mark 16, is included in the narrative, notwithstanding some in our day, for no good reason, have doubted the authenticity of that passage.

In the wisdom of Divine Providence, it is understandable that Marietta should have been chosen for the mission of visiting the opposing worlds which exist on the other side of the grave. True, she possessed unusual talents of expression, and her descriptive power is unrivalled, as indeed to suggest that she was moved by Divine Inspiration. But we speak more especially of the uniqueness of her experiences while she lay in the state of a trance, when she visited both Paradise and the Abyss. Just previously she had been under deep conviction of sin, but because she had vacillated in her faith, she was, at the time she left the body, susceptible to the influence of the prevailing laws of both Paradise and the world of lost spirits. Her nature not having been changed by the experience of the New Birth, she was not able to fully harmonize with heaven's law of harmony. Because of this condition she also felt the influence of the nether world where the prevailing law of evil magnetism reigned. She was permitted for a brief season to enter that dark world and learn its awful secrets, which Christ

3

had once previously sketched in His narrative of the Rich Man in Luke 16. While there she learned the reason why no absolutely discordant souls can ever enter heaven, and indeed if they could, their agony would be intolerable, as they could not endure the harmony and purity of that holy place, and they should find the darkness of the nether regions a welcome alternative.

We also observe that not even angels span the "impassable gulf," but it is indicated that Marietta was rescued from those regions of night by the Lord Jesus Himself.

May the message of Marietta be a solemn warning to all who tread unheeded, the path which leads to death, and who seek happiness in the false pleasures of this sinful world; lest when they leave the body, they be drawn by the law of evil attraction and as a result are plummeted into the abyss of nether darkness—a land where there is no hope. That salvation is provided only through the Great Sacrifice of Calvary, no document has ever presented with more solemn emphasis than Marietta's SCENES BEYOND THE GRAVE.

GORDON LINDSAY

STATEMENT OF ORIGINAL PUBLISHER

The increasing demand for this work, with so little effort to call public attention to it, confirms our first impressions, that it is the Book for the age; one greatly needed to supply the deficiency intuitively sensed by the mind of the present generation.

Edition after edition has been published and passed silently into the hands of the reading public. Reports of an encouraging nature reach us from all sections where it has found its way; and the united testimony of those who avail themselves of the work is, that, to read is to be benefited.

Its sound theology, purely religious sentiment, and thrilling descriptions of scenes enacted beyond the grave, as seen by the spirit of the young girl, while her body lay entranced, cannot, it seems to me, fail to strengthen the faith of the Christian in the truths of Revelation. More particularly is it adapted to the youthful mind of this age, to awaken in it a love of the Christian Religion as it unfolds so graphically the great plan of man's Redemption,— "which things the angels desire to look into."

I have witnessed its effect upon the youthful mind. They, while listening to the thrilling story of Marietta, seem borne along with her enraptured spirit, and with it to witness the unfolding of visions, by which the Infants are being taught to know their Redeemer, that they too, might be able to realize and love Him, who was once a babe in a manger; then a man of sorrows acquainted with grief; then suffering death and triumphing over the grave, for the redemption of a ruined and forlorn race.

I unhesitatingly state it as my firm and unwavering belief, that the spirit of Marietta Davis, like John, the Revelator, while his body was in the Isle of Patmos, visited scenes beyond the grave, and there saw and heard what she relates. However this may be, if the truth can be brought to reach the mind, and win the affections to the Christian Religion, all is gained that should be desired.

STEPHEN DEUEL.

Dayton, O., September 1, 1856.

TABLE OF CONTENTS

CHAPTER   PAGE

I. Introductory Statement 15

II. Man at Death 19

III. City of Peace 24

IV. The Glory of the Cross 29

V. Children in Paradise 33

VI. The Infant Paradise 36

VII. Infants Received by the Savior 41

VIII. Infants Restored to Harmony 45

IX. Christ Revealed as Suffering on the Cross 48

X. The City Viewed from a Superior Plain 52

XI. Marietta Descends to Realms of Darkness 57

XII. The Abode of the Lost 61

XIII. The Abyss—Realm of the Desperately Wicked 71

XIV. Marietta Ascends from the Abyss 82

XV. Marietta Learns of Her Unfitness to Enjoy
     Heaven 87

XVI. The Forlorn and Doomed Being 93

XVII. The Babe of Bethlehem 100

XVIII. Justice and Mercy 103

XIX. The Betrayal 108

XX. Cruelties Inflicted Upon Jesus 117

XXI. Christ Before Tribunal 122

XXII. The Dream of Pilate's Wife 127

XXIII. Jesus Led Out to Be Crucified 130

XXIV. Judas Repenting 137

XXV. Calvary 143

XXVI. Death of the Savior 147

XXVII. The Resurrection and Ascension 154

XXVIII. The Rescue 160

XXIX. Marietta's Return to Earth 164

TESTIMONY AUTHENTICATING
THE VISION

The following testimonials from the mother and sisters of Marietta Davis; and from Emerson Hull, M.D., who had been a resident of Berlin for many years, and is a physician of eminence, are but a part of those in possession of the editor, but are considered sufficient to authenticate the narrative.

1. Testimony of the Family.

Berlin, New York, Nov. 15, 1855.

Rev. J. L. Scott:

Dear Friend:—Since you have been publishing the trance of Marietta Davis, in the Mountain Cove Journal, some of the readers have written to us to ascertain its authenticity. Upon this account, and to relieve you from embarrassment, we submit the following for your disposal:

Marietta Davis was a member of our family;—she was born in this town, where she lived until called by death from us.

She was not of open religious habits; being disinclined to religious conversation. During the revival in the winter of 1847-'8, her mind, as you well know, was religiously exercised; but she could not realize what others professed, so as to enable her to unite with her young friends in the ordinances of the Gospel. In August following she fell into a sleep, or trance, from which she could not be awakened.—In that state she remained nine days; and when she awoke, she said she had been in Heaven; that she had seen there many of her old friends and relations who were dead; and Jesus the Redeemer. From that time her hope in heaven through Jesus, was strong; and she rejoiced in the prospect of a final admission into the Paradise of Peace.

During her short stay with us, after she came out of the trance, she related what she said she had seen, heard and learned during her sleep; but much of what she told us, she said she wished should not be mentioned then, for the world was not prepared to hear it. The trance, as you published it, as far as we can recollect, is correct; only you have omitted much. Marietta fell asleep in August, 1848, and died the following March, and at the time and in the manner predicted by herself.

Yours,
Nancy Davis, Mother,
Susan Davis, Sister,
Sarah Ann Davis, Sister.

2. TESTIMONY OF ATTENDING PHYSICIAN.

Berlin, New York, Nov. 15, 1853.
Rev. J. L. Scott:

Dear Sir:—In the summer of 1848, with yourself, I visited the widow Nancy Davis, of this town, in the capacity of medical attendant upon her daughter Marietta, who had fallen into a state of catalepsy, or trance, in which she remained nine days, and from which to awaken her human skill seemed unavailing. When she returned to her normal state, she related much of a remarkable character, which she said she had learned while in the trance.

Having read portions of what you have published in the Mountain Cove Journal, I am prepared to give my testimony as to its strict correspondence to what I heard her relate before her death.

Your Obedient Servant,
EMERSON HULL, M.D.

3. Testimony of Prominent Ministers Living at Time of Vision.

Lest some who have not read this Trance, and are therefore unacquainted with its character, should class it with books "got up" by the "spirit media" of the day, and to assure the reader that its correct sentiment and pure spirit commend it to the confidence of the Religious Public, we insert the following statements of the Rev. Mr. Waller, of Kentucky, and the Rev. Mr. Miller, of Springfield, Ohio.

Rev. G. Waller, one of the first ministers of the Baptist order, in Kentucky, whose sound Theology and good sense won him, for twenty-five consecutive years, the highest office in his denomination, and whose name is sufficient commendation for any Work through the wide field of his usefulness, and wherever his name is known, writes as follows:

"I have carefully examined a book bearing the title: "Scenes Beyond the Grave," purporting to be a simple narrative of scenes enacted beyond the grave, and witnessed by the spirit of a young girl while she lay entranced, as the testimony shows. Of this I express no opinion; but fully approve of its pure and deep-toned spirit of Christianity, and sound Theology.

"The Scenes are so truly depicted, and so beautifully and thrillingly told, that it cannot fail to secure the judgment, and win the confidence and affections of all who read it.

"I am constrained to say, that in purity of style, and richness of composition, it is not excelled by any work I have read. I should be pleased if it could be placed upon the table of every family, and read in every common and Sunday school in the land. Infidelity can have little influence where it is read. It is particularly adapted to the use of families and schools, to form in the young mind the first impressions. I therefore, very cheerfully recommend it to the public, and particularly to all who love the Bible and the Christian religion."

GEORGE WALLER.

Louisville, Ky., June 15, 1855.

Rev. Mr. Miller, of Springfield, Ohio, Minister of the Methodist Episcopal Church, a man of deep devotion and marked piety who has not only the confidence of his Church, but for some twenty years has held a responsible office—the gift of the people of his City and County—in a letter speaks thus:

Rev. J. L. Scott:—

"I have before me the first part of the Trance of Marietta Davis, entitled "Scenes Beyond the Grave," which I have read with inexpressible delight; and it so far exceeds any work I have previously read, which treats upon the lost state of man, and his redemption through our Lord Jesus Christ, that I am constrained to urge upon you the necessity of placing it in the hands of every family in the land.

"Its richness, and purity of style, its poetic grandeur and figurative excellence, so possess the mind of the reader, that he seems himself 'entranced,' and borne far beyond the darkness and imperfections of earth, to be an observer with the spirit of Marietta, of the lovely scenes that occupy the inhabitants of heaven; and also as was revealed to her, the reader realizes most deeply the depth of iniquity into which man is fallen by reason of sin, and becomes lost in the contemplation of the boundless goodness bestowed in his redemption.

"Her description, as revealed to her, of the display of Justice, and Mercy, the meekness, love and suffering of the Savior, in the purpose and completion of the plan of Salvation, is unequalled; and the narrative of what she saw in Paradise, where the infants from earth are received, agreeing so perfectly as it does with our highest hopes of the blessedness of our little ones, who have departed this life, fills the reader with ecstacy.

"No language of mine is in any way capable of explaining the feelings that awaken in the soul, while reading the narrative, and whatever may have been the

inspiring cause (and I believe she saw what she relates),
I feel that whoever reads the Trance with any degree of
care will receive from it, lasting benefit.

"I am therefore solicitous that it should be spread
abroad through the land, and the more especially, since
it is so well calculated to counteract the destructive influence of that Infidelity, now so abundantly promul-
gated, by the advocates of modern Infidel Spiritualism.
In the bonds of Christian affection,

I am yours,

REUBEN MILLER.

Springfield, Clark Co., O., June 9, 1855.

4. Testimony of Marietta's Pastor.

The work now presented to the public as depicting
"Scenes Beyond the Grave," does not come without
authority for its somewhat startling title. In the summer
of 1848, a young woman named Marietta Davis, aged
twenty-five years, residing with her mother Mrs. Nancy
Davis, at Berlin, New York, fell into a sleep or trance,
in which she remained for nine days. All endeavors on
the part of her friends and of her physicians failed to
arouse her from this unnatural state. When at last she
awoke to a consciousness of external things, she was in
the full possession of all her natural faculties, with an
almost supernatural acuteness of perception superadded.

Before she fell into the trance, her mind had been
considerably exercised in regard to her future state; but
there was yet a lingering doubt which greatly disturbed
her. Her mother and sisters were exemplary members of
a Baptist Church, in Berlin, then under my pastoral
charge, but Marietta's doubt seemed to have kept her
from the enjoyment of the hope in which her family
so confidently rested. But when she came out of the

trance, in which she had lain for so many days, it was with joy and rejoicing over the unspeakable things which she had seen and heard. Her mouth was filled with praises to God, and her heart swelled with gratitude to Him for His loving kindness. She averred that while her body lay as it were in death, her spirit had visited the eternal world. She informed her friends that she was not to remain long with them: but should soon go hence to enjoy a mansion prepared for her in her heavenly Father's Kingdom. After this she lived seven months and died at the time predicted by herself; and so perfectly did she know the hour of her departure, that when it arrived she selected a hymn and commenced singing it with the family; and while they sang, her spirit took its flight so gently as not to attract attention. Thus the hymn commenced with her friends on earth, was doubtless concluded with the angels in heaven.

The style of Marietta's narrative is peculiar. She regretted her inability to express her conceptions of what she had seen and heard, so as to give a definite idea of the glories of the heavenly world. I have not felt at liberty to change the style of her narrative, and as far as possible have employed her own language. Having received the story from her own lips, I have so preserved it, as to make it in truth the relation of her own experience.

The tone of the trance is exalted and Christlike; and therefore its influence cannot fail to be of a useful and sacred character. Confident of this, I offer it to the public. If read in the spirit in which it was given, it cannot fail to gladden and encourage the Christian, and to lead the thoughts of the man of the world beyond his material existence. For while following her in her wide range of spiritual thoughts and visions, forgetting the outer world, we fancy that the heavens are opened to our view, revealing their glory and magnificence. We seem to see the moving multitudes, who with golden harps and angelic voices are chanting praises to God. With ecstacy we behold, as mirrored before us, the Infant Paradise; and appear ourselves to be observing the order and harmony of the inhabitants of that divine sphere. Then borne onward and upward by her entrancing story, in the spirit we seem to arise with saints and angels and become familiar with the inhabitants of the Celestial Heavens, and are led to exclaim, "Marietta! thou favored of Heaven, we bless that Providence which unfolded thy vision, while we read with delight of soul, the revelations of thy entranced spirit!"

J. L. SCOTT.

SCENES BEYOND THE GRAVE

Chapter I

INTRODUCTORY STATEMENT

There are no means to convey to man through his external senses, any just idea of the scenes I witnessed, while my body was reposing in its unconscious slumbers. No medium of communication is sufficiently clear, to give the perfect outlines of that which is invisible and incomprehensible to mortals. For human utterance mars the beauty and perfection of heavenly speech, and corrupts the purity of thoughts thus conveyed. You urge me to a history, and yet I am so sensible of my utter inability that thoughts associated with the attempt give me pain.

Her Longing for Knowledge of Immortality

Long had I discovered the vanity of earthly things, the imperfections of human associations, the unreliability of vast portions of religious faiths and impressions, and the want of permanent peace in the disquieted soul of man. Most earnestly I desired to know more of the reality of that state called by mortals immortality. At length, meditating from day to day, and while laboring to determine the nature and tendency of the human soul, I became less conscious of external things, and my inner mind grew stronger and more active, until the dim shadows of the objects and interests of this busy life of mortals ceased with the expiring view, and my vision closed to the outer world.

Her Spirit Leaves the Body

Then objects new and strange appeared. Still I knew not that I was retiring from the world of sorrow and of human strife; nor did I understand that my spiritual vision was opening, and what I saw dimly moving before me was a reality, the dawning of an immortal life. Still I seemed to be departing from some former condition and launching out into a boundless sea, and to be traversing unexplored regions, veiled in uncertain vision, and floating in mid air over an immeasurable deep below. Alone and unguided, and possessed of a vague uncertainty, my timid spirit fain would have returned to the land of shadows whence it came.

An Angel Meets Her

Half-conscious of my present condition, with dreamy thoughts, I seemed to ask, is there no one familiar with the journey I pursue, to guide me in my movements through this trackless space? When lo! in the distance, and above me, I saw a light descending, having the appearance of a brilliant star. As it advanced, its foreshadowing halo illumined the expanse about me, and my exhausted being received new life from the invigorating glory that beamed upon it. Gently I began to move, and ascending, drew nearer the source of that light which gladdened and quickened my spirit. As I approached it, I began to discover the outlines of what appeared to me a glorified human being; gradually the figure became more distinct, until, poised in the atmosphere before and above me, was an angel, whose excellence far exceeded the highest conception of the fairest image of my human thought. That form, more lovely than languages hath power to portray, moved silently as it drew near me. Upon her head was a crown, formed like gems of clustering rays. In her left hand was a cross, emblem of meekness, innocence and redeeming grace; in her right hand a wand of pure intellectual light. With this she touched my lips, and like a flame of holy love, it quickened an immortal principle which diffused its enlivening spirit throughout my being. A new class of sensations awoke within me, and moving harmoniously, prompted a desire for companionship with the angelic being. I looked upon her, wishing to learn her name, when lo! she spoke. She said: "Marietta, thou desirest to know me. In my errand to thee I am called the Angel of Peace. I come to guide thee where those exist who are from earth, whence thou art. Wouldst thou profit by the lesson, follow me. But first behold thy form in yonder world." There, far below me, and through a dark and misty way, I beheld this sickly body of mortality. Around it were gathered my anxious friends, employing every means to awaken it, but all in vain.

A View of a Dying World

"Behold," said my glorious guide, "a picture of human life. There, kindred, tortured with sympathetic love, struggle to hold the crumbling vase, and keep the flickering light from expiring. There, from youth to hoary age, rolls the tide of human woe. Fond hearts are severed. Death veils from mortal sight the tender, lovely form. The opening flower that gladdens all around, folds its expanding leaves, withered with the touch of death. There, hopes, like dreamy phantoms, float in the mid-air of fancied bliss. As thy vision expandeth, witness thou the moving hosts. Earth, with her swarming millions, presents a mingled scene of rising hopes, ambition, strife and death. Her inhabitants are dismayed by the approach and fear of Death, the fell destroyer. Time quickly measureth the fleeting moments of human existence, and generations follow generations in quick succession."

To this address I replied, "These thoughts are the burden of my young and inexperienced mind. These forms thou hast shown me, are before my vision. Like dew drops they pass away. This is the cause of my sorrow. Canst thou tell me in what portion of the universe these beings find a resting place when their spirits depart? Canst thou remove the veil that conceals them from mortal vision? Canst thou guide me where they are? O! tell me, have they a home, or a place, and may I follow where my loved ones have been borne?"

Chapter II

MAN AT DEATH

"Wouldst thou know the condition of the departed members of thy race, and be made familiar with the effects of the habits and associations of perverted man? Measurably thou mayest; but know thou that their conditions are varied." Then bidding me look upward she said, "What beholdest thou?" Obedient, I looked above me, and with wonder beheld an orb brighter by far than the sun of earth in its meridian glory. Light, pure, beaming along the celestial skies, radiated therefrom.— "There," said my guide, "are many thou wouldst see, who, clothed in raiment soft and white, move in harmony. There, night-shades never fall, and death and gloom have no element. Those who enjoy that blest abode do not suffer; no sin or pain disturbs their calm repose. But more of this thou shalt hereafter learn. Other scenes less joyous must first be given thee. Marietta, thou knowest well, that with man are varied characters. *The departure of the spirit from its unsettled and shattered habitation below, worketh no change in its nature.*" Then touching my forehead, again she said, "What seest thou?" My vision being opened to a new scene, I beheld before me forms without number, struggling in the agonies of death. Some in kingly palaces on dying couches richly hung with drapery of costly price. Some in humble cottages; others in gloomy prisons; haunts of vice and iniquity; lone forests; barren deserts, and in deep and wild waters. Some lying beneath the scorching sun; some perishing upon bleak and snowy mountains; some surrounded with weeping and attentive friends; others dying alone and forgotten. Some expiring from wounds inflicted by the assassin; others crushed beneath the heavy tread of the war-horse in the battle-field.

Effects of the Violated Law

Thus where time and eternity meet, was revealed a scene of indescribable misery. "This," said my guide, "is but a faint view of the effects of violated law."

Touched again by the light beaming from her right hand, I beheld the immortality of those who were quitting their house of clay, entering upon the regions of eternity and commencing new and untried realities. Around each dying form were gathered spirits, varied in appearance and in movement.

Man at Death Gravitates to His Own Place

Over battle-fields were congregated spirits of the dead, and according to the moral nature of the dying, was that of attending spirits who awaited their arrival in the spirit world. In like manner, all classes and conditions are effected, since this intermediate state or vestibule of the spirit world, is visited by beings varying in character from the unholy and wretched, to the bright and sanctified angels who in multitudes congregate at the portals of death, as messengers of God. And all classes as they emerge from the physical form are attracted to and mingle with kindred associations, beings to whose character they assimilate. *Those of discordant and unhallowed natures are attracted by like elements, and enter into regions overhung with clouds of night; while those, who for the love of good, desire pure associations, are by heavenly messengers conducted to the orb of glories appearing above the intermediate scene.*

The strange sensations of human spirits as they mingled with the disembodied multitudes, beholding what was transpiring around them, excited my wonder, and while watching their movements, I began to ask myself, if what I saw was a reality or mere imagery reflected upon my mind in a dreamy state? Upon discovering my thoughts, my guide took me by the hand saying, "These beings moving about thee, once the inhabitants of earth whence thou art, having left their mortal dwellings, are commencing a new state of existence. Their surprise is the effect of their sudden change from external objects and sense to spiritual, and their more immediate knowledge of cause and effect. But more of this state and their condition shall be revealed, when that instruction will better befit thy mind. These scenes we will leave and ascend to yon bright orb." Thus saying she led me toward the cloud of light.

While passing the intermediate she touched me again, and I became conscious of additional and expanded vision.

"Behold," said she, "the countless, planetary hosts. Mark the rolling orbs, suns, and systems of suns, moving in silence and harmony. *The vast expanse is occupied and peopled with universes, constructed in infinite wisdom. These are inhabited by holy beings, happy and immortal, though varied in degree of development and refined spirituality.*"

The Ministry of Angels

Again the organs of perception were touched, and lo! above and around me, and far in the distance, were passing and repassing with the quickness of thought, spirits of pure light.

"These," said my guide, "are ministering angels; their supreme delight is to go upon errands of mercy. Their home is with the ever blest. They are employed as guardian protectors and messengers to those in conditions below them."

While beholding them ascend and descend, one drew near me, in whose arms, and borne upon whose angelic bosom, was an infant spirit. The angel passed, and I saw that the nourished nestling rested in calm security, ap-

parently conscious of its safety in the hands of its protector. "Whence came this?" I inquired; and the angel answered, "I received it from a heart-broken mother at the
gateway of death, as the spark of life expired in the
external world, and am conveying it to the sphere of
infancy in the paradise of peace."

Entering Paradise

As the infant's guardian spirit proceeded, we moved
silently in the same direction, until the scenes below
perished from my vision, and my being was absorbed in
the bright light descending from the orb we were approaching. Soon we entered a plain, whereon were visible
trees, bearing fruit. Passing through these shadowy,
groves, I was delighted with the melody of the birds,
whose warbling notes arose in sweetest song. There we
paused. Supposing that I was on some terrestrial orb I
inquired its name.

My guide answered, "These trees, these flowers, these
birds occupy the outer expanse of the spiritual paradise.
So pure are they, and so refined, that mortals with be-
clouded vision may not behold them. And so soft their
notes that they are not made audible to the dull hearing
of men. Beings inhabiting forms more gross, do not con-
ceive the reality of the existence of nature so refined.
Absent from thy body, thou canst comprehend through
spiritual senses the existence and reality of spiritual habitations; but what thou dost now behold is but the outline
and more exterior of the home of spirits. These floral
plains, and warbling melodies, are but the lower order of
the external habitation of the sanctified.

"Here the redeemed are first conducted by their
guardian protectors, as they leave the valley and shadow
of death, and here they are taught the rudiments of immortal life. Here they receive instructive lessons relative

to their heavenly abode, and learn the nature of pure love, unmarred by sin. Here friends who have advanced in spiritual attainments return from higher employment to welcome the spirit on its entrance upon this plane of the spirit world. Here kindred are permitted to meet and hold converse; and 'tis in these immortal groves where spirits first attempt in unity the song of redeeming grace, and reposing in soft and heavenly sweetness, breathe the pure air of paradise."

While listening to this strange, though welcome address, my spirit burned to meet the friends long lost to me on earth. The angel said, "Thou art not to tarry, since thy present mission is to learn the condition of the departed child of God. When thy course on earth is ended, here thou shalt mingle in the infancy of thy immortal state, with thy kindred and receive lessons, preparatory to an advance to more exalted mansions, the more glorified home of the blessed."

Then she reached out her hand, and plucked a rose that hung over us, and bidding me receive its fragrance, with it touched my lips. Again a more interior sight was given, and I beheld around me, and moving in every direction, through the varied floral scenes, happy beings without number. Desiring to mingle with them, I sought permission; but my guide moved on, and upward through forests becoming more pure and fair as we ascended.

Chapter III

CITY OF PEACE

At a distance, I saw a dome of light. "That," said my guide, "is the gateway leading to the City of Peace. There the manifestation of thy Redeemer is made visible. There saints and angels abide; on harps of gold, and stringed instruments, with immortal lyres, in alleluias, chant the Song of Redemption; the song of peace; the song of love undying."

As we drew near, a class of attendants, more glorious, gathered around the gateway, and one foremost addressed my guide in language I could not understand. A gate of jasper, set with diamonds, opened, and two angelic beings approached, and taking me by each hand, led my tremulous spirit towards and inner gate, a more immediate entrance to the pavillion of light.

Marietta Meets The Redeemer

Then I remembered my discordant state; then thoughts of my former sins, my doubts, and rebellious nature, rushed upon my mind, and feeling entirely unprepared to endure the glory of the assemblage, my spirit failed me. The angelic attendants then bore me in their arms along the portal to the feet of a being most glorious. Upon his head was a crown of pure light, and over his shoulders hung golden locks! His loveliness, can never be expressed.

"This, Marietta," said an attending angel, "is thy Redeemer. For thee in incarnation he suffered. For thee without the gate treading the winepress alone, he expired." Awed by his goodness, tenderness and love, I bowed, feeling that if worthy I would worship him.

Reaching forth his hand he raised me up, and in a voice that filled my soul with inexpressible delight, said, "Welcome, my child. Daughter, spirit of a race forlorn, enter thou for a season the portals of the redeemed." Then addressing the surrounding beings, continued, "Receive this your companion spirit." And lo! the worshiping congregation arose as upon the breath of holy love, and, meekly welcomed me as an heir of grace, and with tuned instruments the immortal choir chanted the spirit's welcome—

"Worthy is the Lamb who hath redeemed us. Exalt His name, all ye sanctified, yea adore Him, ye cherubim who worship in the celestial heavens. Adore Him, for He hath exalted us. We will praise His name, the name of our God Most High."

The music of this soft and melodious utterance, moved like the voice of many waters, filling the entire dome, and as the anthem closed, the echo departed in the distance, as though borne from wave to wave, along the holy atmosphere.

She Meets Loved Ones

Each measure like noiseless waves swelled over that sea of mind; and with their gentle undulations I seemed to be moving when a spirit from the innumerable company approached and addressing me in a familiar manner called me by name.

The spell of music being broken, I was much affected to find myself in the embrace of one who on earth I had loved with the affection of an infant soul. With willingness I sank into her arms, and she with a sister's tenderness pressed me to her immortal form, saying, "Sister spirit, welcome, for a season to our home of peace."

"Thrice welcome," uttered the music of a thousand voices, and lo! around me gathered those I loved, all eager to greet me, and receive me to their kind embrace.

Around us, and in this spacious room, appeared seats in form of an amphitheatre, yet glorious beyond description. Hereon we rested. Mingling with them, were many old and familiar friends.

Although I knew them, their appearance was unlike that while upon earth, each being an embodiment of intellect unassociated with the physical form, in which I had known them before. Not having power, or any means adapted to convey a just idea, I can only give feeble utterance to my conceptions of their nature by saying, they appeared all mind, all light, all glory, all adoration, all love supremely pure, all peace and calm serenity, all united in sublime employ, all expression of heavenly unfolding joy.

Freely did they converse, nor did they use the language of human beings. They spoke and no audible utterance attended, yet thought moved with thought, and spirit was familiar with the mind of spirit. Ideas associated with their heavenly life, flowed from being to being, *and soon I learned that in heaven there is no concealment.* Harmony of soul, harmony of desire, harmony of speech, harmony in the swelling notes of adoring anthems, harmony was their life, their love, their manifestation, and supreme delight.

Again with harps tuned in unison, they chanted a hymn to their Maker's name. My guide urged me to unite in the animating song of redemption. I could not join them, being absorbed in the contemplation and glory of this long-sought home of rest. When they closed that sacred hymn, my guide, touching my lips again with the wand of light, bade me mingle, a companion, with the members of this divine abode.

Being after being pressed to mine, immortal lips, and seemed anxious to fold me in their arms. As a soul, new-born, they caressed me, after looking up in thankfulness to their Redeemer and their Lord.

"And is this Heaven?" my spirit said. "Are these happy souls those who once struggled in forms of clay? Are these immortal visages, radiant with the glory of this adoring mansion, the spiritual countenances of those I have before seen in careworn life? And where has fled that age and decreptitude, ye parent spirits?"

Often have I listened to you, my earthly teacher, while laboring to convey to the understandings of your audience, some faint idea of your conceptions of immortal life. Often have I discovered manifest grief when in spirit you appeared to realize that upon most minds all was but an ineffectual effort. And then I have asked, can heaven be thus glorious? is not the picture too highly wrought? and may man, if he attain to that blest abode, bask in the sunbeams of such supreme delight? *And be assured, the highest thoughts of man fail to approach the reality and the delights of that heavenly scene.*

The Pilgrim's Address

Then approached me one whom on earth I had seen bending tremulously over the pilgrim's staff. I knew 'twas one familiar, one of age and emaciated form, whose hoary head once told the story of a life of woe. In immortal youth the spirit stood before me; no staff was there; no trembling frame, no grief-worn cheek, no hollow eye, no sickly form; but light and health and vigor were manifest. And the spirit said, "Behold in me the efficacy of redeeming grace. This heart was once the cage of thoughts unholy. These hands were employed in sin. These feet moved swiftly in the downward road that led to sorrow and to death. This form of mine, though not this form, yet that in which I used to live, was worn with grief, corrupt and dying with disease. But now, all hail that name, Immanuel! through Him, redeemed, I wear habiliments of light and exist in immortal youth. This song I chant, 'O death, where is thy sting? and grave, thy victory now? Worthy is the Lamb who offered Himself to redeem! Worthy—O give Him adoration, ye countless hosts, ye innumerable throng! Worship and adore Him, all intelligences! yea, let the universes adore! Adore Him, for He is worthy to receive anthems of universal praise!' "

Then appeared a company of children, who hand in hand, moved around and their infant voices chanted: "Praise Him, for lo! While on earth He said, 'Suffer infants to come to me and forbid them not; yea, suffer little children, and forbid them not, to come unto me.' "

CHAPTER IV

THE GLORY OF THE CROSS

When this new song was ended, I looked and lo! the dome above me parted, and beings far more glorious approached. Awed by the presence of the light, I approached my guide, who said, "What thou hast seen, Marietta, is but the earnest of joys to come. Here thou hast been welcomed, and here witnessed this manifestation of thy Redeemer. But, behold! above thee the descending glory of the Cross appears. Spirits, members of thy race, redeemed, who are advanced to higher life, attend.

The Cross Appears

Then visible above me appeared a Cross, borne in the midst of twelve, on whose circle I read, "Patriarchs, Prophets and Apostles." Above it was written, "Jesus of Nazareth, King of the Jews." Bowing at the feet was a spirit, whose raiment was white, and expression that of holy adoration. She kissed the Cross, and then descending, approached me, and said, "Welcome spirit from the world of woe. Lo! by the will of Jesus, even that Jesus crucified, my Lord and Redeemer, I come to commune with thee. 'Tis but by his permission thou art admitted here; and be not sad, though thou shouldst be required to return to thy friends on earth."

A Divine Purpose In Marietta's Visit to Paradise

The thought of being subjected again to the sins and misfortunes of my former life, so affected me that it seemed as if I was quitting the divine abode, and rapidly descending to earth; when lo! I was embraced by my guide, who said, "When thou returnest, thou shalt go to bear a message of holy love, to earth; and at an appointed time, free from the power of mortal attachments, thou shalt enter here, a member of the holy band."

The spirit who descended from the Cross then said, "Marietta, thou hast been conducted here for a wise end, and for that purpose I am permitted to instruct thee in many things, pertaining to earth and heaven. The thought of returning makes thee sad; yet thou shalt go laden with riches, the riches of instructive truth.

Guardian Angels

"First learn that all Heaven reveres the Cross. Before it myriads bow, and around it the redeemed delight to linger. Earth's religions are but dreamy scenes, compared to these. Vague and imperfect are the highest conceptions of the human soul, relative to our condition here. 'Tis but just above the plains of earth, where in perfect order begins the Spiritual Heaven. Around it move the guardian spirits. Mingling, as permitted, with the inhabitants of earth are countless guardian angels; no day, nor hour, nor moment passeth, but each mortal is watched by the spirit appointed to his charge.

The Second Coming of Christ Draws Near

"Man knoweth not the nature of sin, nor the fullness of Grace in his Redemption. Numberless are the causes, to prevent the light of heaven from reaching and controlling the race of man, wretched and deathward tending. But the time draweth near, when man shall become more conscious of the reality of this abode; when his attention shall be turned more fully to the truth of Inner Life. *Man's redemption draweth nigh. Let angels swell the chorus; for soon the Savior descendeth, with holy attending angels.*"

Then after an immortal hymn, she said, "Observe what passeth around thee; for lo! shall be mirrored upon thy mind a faint expression of the joy that fills this land of peace. Thou didst notice when I descended, I kissed the Cross. All saints delight themselves in thus expressing their remembrance and regard for their Redeemer who offered himself a sacrifice."

A pause in the address ensued, during which, voices, apparently in the distance, arose in soft and melodious alleluias.

"Who are these?" I inquired. "These are they," she said, "who having come out of great tribulation, cease not day nor night to raise their anthems high, in exaltation of their Savior's name.

Marietta Receives a Gentle Reproof

"Wouldst thou dwell for ever in this world of peace, joy and love divine? Wouldst thou bear some humble part with the psalms of these immortal choralists? Be thou admonished by thy former incredulity, thy want of faith and consecration; for *there are no other means than those in Christ, the Redeemer, by which to attain inheritance in this blest abode.*"

This last address revived within me remembrance of my former doubts, my want of confidence in the Savior, and of consecration to his cause. My spirit drooped. I saw the justice of the mild reproof, and inquired, "May I yet hope? Or is the opportunity to secure this heaven of life forever gone? Fain would I return no more to earth. O, that I could forever dwell where peace like a river gently floweth, and love unpolluted, moveth from heart to heart!"

The Scene of the Prophets and Martyred Saints

"Be faithful, then," said the spirit, "to the light given, and at last thou shalt enjoy the bliss of heaven. Marietta, the scene now passing before thee, is one fraught with interest. In this assembly are the Prophets and martyred

Saints. See, their raiment is white, pure and transparent. Upon their breast is the manifestation of the Cross. In their left hand is a golden censer, and in their right a small volume."

The scene expanded and I saw that from the centre, and around which the multitudes were congregated, arose a pyramid whose column was composed of pearls and most precious stones, set with crosses of spiritualized diamond, upon which were engraven the names of those who had suffered for their love of Truth, and who not counting their lives dear, had endured persecution even unto death. Upon this column stood three spirits, in the attitude of meekness and adoration, holding in their hand, and above them a Cross from which floated a banner ever unfurling,—"These," said my guide, "are select, one Patriarch, one Prophet, and one Apostle. *They represent the triune circle of commissioned saints who shall attend the reappearing of the Son of Man, and shall go forth in the day appointed, gathering together the elect from the four winds, from the uttermost part of the earth to the uttermost part of heaven.*"

"The volumes the spirits hold in their hands unfold the order of creation, the redemption of man, and the principles which govern the obedient, world without end."

CHAPTER V

CHILDREN IN PARADISE

As the former scene closed upon my view, the spirit who kissed the Cross, raised her hand, radiant with the light of life, and two children drew near. As they approached, they bowed gracefully, and each placing a hand in hers, with meekness looked into her lovely face and smiled.

Addressing me she said, "These children left the form while in their infancy, and being innocent, were conducted to paradise.

The eldest of the two, thus introduced, said, "Marietta, I rejoice to commune with thee, since thou shalt return to those who loved us and who mourned our departure from the valley of death.

"When thou art again conversing with mortals, say to him who now sits by thy body, that we have learned that though parents may grieve for us, ours is a cup overflowing with gladness to the spirit made free.

"Marietta, this is the world we know. Here we first awoke to the reality of our existence. Earth we visit, conducted by our guardian angels, but it is unlike heaven. There we witness sorrow, pain and death; here, harmony, happiness and life abide."

He then looked down as if in deep meditation and all was silent. I thought the subject which had engaged his mind, had made him sad, but soon saw that his attitude was occasioned by the approach of an angel who in ascending had passed just above us. O, how my being was affected at the sight! Light surrounded her as a well wrought garment. Her very movement was the harmony of harmonies. I desired to follow, and said, "O tell me, who is this so glorious? I feel her sacred influence, and ardently desire to enjoy the society and the abode of such beings."

Angel Carries Infant to Paradise

"This," said the spirit, "is an angel who belongs to the Infant Paradise. Have you not read in the Gospel, that blessed expression of the Redeemer, "In heaven their angels always behold the face of their Heavenly Father? This angel has the guardian protection of infants, and is commissioned to meet infant spirits as they leave the external world and enter into the spiritual. She pauses in her ascension for thee. She holds out her arms, and what seest thou, Marietta?" "A small pale light," I answered.

The angel then breathed upon it, as if imparting life, and pressed it to her bosom in fondness infinitely above that manifested by earthly mothers. I knew the little spirit was at rest. Feeling the heaven that encompassed and pervaded the angel, again I wished to fly away, and with the infant be forever blessed. But while I was struggling to ascend, the angel arose—one flash of light and she disappeared.

The Sorrowing Mother on Earth

Then a far different scene was revealed—below me in a little room, I saw a female kneeling by the lifeless body of her departed child. She convulsed, and at times tears streamed from her eyes, and then her face was as marble, her eyes set and glassy, and her whole form quivered while she pressed kiss after kiss upon the cold cheek of her lost babe. At this juncture a man dressed in black gravely entered. The group gave way and he silently approached the weeping mother, and taking her by the hand said, "Sister arise. The Lord gave and the

Lord hath taken away, blessed be the name of the Lord. Jesus said, 'Suffer little children to come unto me and forbid them not, for of such is the kingdom of heaven. For I say unto you, their angels always behold the face of their Heavenly Father.' "

Next I saw that mother, sitting beside a coffin, in an earthly assemblage. Her eye was fixed upon the ceiling. Her countenance wore an expression of despair. Before the coffin stood the grave looking man, whom I had seen enter the room of death. He read a Psalm, offered prayer for the afflicted, and then encouraged the mourners, by endeavoring to prove from the sacred text, that the babe, though dead shall live again, and that an angel had conveyed it to Abraham's bosom.

The assembly disappeared, and the child addressed me saying, "The lifeless form just seen in the vision, was the representation of my own body, the weeping mother was my own mother; the scene was that which transpired when I left that body; the grave man was the minister of a congregation in the outer world.

"The angel who while passing us paused, was the bright spirit who conveyed me far above the influence of evil magnetism, to a place prepared for the young and delicate infant, where spirits appointed, are ever occupied in nourishing infant minds. Dost thou wish to visit that nursery?" Thus saying he looked up to the spirit, as if to ask permission to conduct me there.

CHAPTER **VI**

THE INFANT PARADISE

In a moment we were ascending in the direction of the angel who had borne along the infant, and who had disappeared in the light. Soon we drew near that which at first appeared like a city built in the midst of a floral plain. There appeared stately edifices and streets lined with trees whose foliage cast a lovely shade; on whose branches birds of all colors appeared; and although all were singing with different notes, all mingled in one full and perfect harmony. Many corresponded to those on earth, and yet were as superior to them as the Paradise itself was superior to the mortal world.

As we advanced, the beauty and harmony increased, and new scenes appeared. The architecture of the edifices, the sculptures in the open air, the fountains that sparkled in the light, the trees that waved their extended branches, the flowers and flowering vines becoming more majestic, interwoven and beautiful. There were also many avenues, each of which, slightly ascending, led to a common center toward which we pursued our way.

Instruction of Infants

As we advanced, I perceived before me a vast and complicated structure, whose outer walls and towers appeared formed of marble, that was in appearance delicate as snow. This served as the foundation of a vast canopy, like a dome, though far too extended to be expressed by the earthly architectural meaning of that term. We drew near this building, and I perceived that the dome was suspended over the vast circular space. "This," said my guide, "is the place where all infants from thy globe are gathered for the instruction. There infants are first conducted, and there nourished beneath the smile of their guardian angels. Each nursery, though somewhat varying, is a miniature of this vast temple of instructive manifestation, and each is a home for the infant spirits who enter there, until they attain to higher degrees, and enter the Paradise of more advanced youthful existence, for degrees of instruction adapted to a more intellectual condition. Over each of these are appointed seven maternal guardians. Thou seest, Marietta, that no two edifices are perfectly alike in interior beauty, external form or decoration, but that all harmoniously combine; and also, that each guardian angel is different in the radiative light and individuality of the faces and form. This thou art permitted to know.

Classification of Infants

"Whenever an infant dies on earth, the angel guardian who bears up the spirit to the Land of Peace, perceives its interior type of mind, and according to its type it is classed with others of like order of intelligence; and as the skillful gardener on earth in one floral division trains the various species of the lily, and in another compartment roses, and in another the camellias or the honeysuckles; so here angelic wisdom classifies the infant spirits, and according to their variety of artistic, scientific, and social tendencies, assigneth each a home best adapted to the unfolding of its interior germs of life, into intellectual, artistic or industrial harmony.

"Over each edifice preside seven guardian angels, who collectively form one octavo of instruction, each angel being of that type of mind which agrees with his associates, as one note harmonizes with the associate tones and semi-tones of the harmonic scale.

"The infants are led forth each day, or each successive period corresponding thereto, to the centre pavilion, for the education of their unfolding natures. As soon as these infants arise to a degree suitable for the general assembly in the great and centre dome, or temple of instruction, they are led first from their several homes to their separate centre school, and then all emerge from the different wards and move beneath a cloud of angel choralists, who chant loud alleluias to their Prince and Savior, and with whose harmony the infants move toward the outer temple."

A School in Paradise

As the spirit closed, I saw on our right a portion of one of the lesser temples remove, as if an invisible hand gathered it in a manner corresponding to the removal of a suspended curtain, and lo! to my already astonished spirit, there appeared visible the interior of one of the nurseries, supremely light with the glory thereof, and adorned with artistic beauty correspondent to the majestic appearance of the paradise of infants. At first I was greatly abashed, feeling my own unfitness to behold any abode so pure, lovely and majestic. "There," I unconsciously uttered, "is heaven." My reflections were perceived by my instructress who observed, "Marietta, behold the manifestation of infant life in Paradise. Let us enter, and there thou shalt learn the true condition of those who as babes leave the world of sorrow, and who are immediately conveyed to this place and are henceforth happy. Little do mortals know of the blessedness attending their little ones who leave in the morning of their existence. Those who believe in Christ, become reconciled to the loss, but this is mostly upon condition of the law of submission established in the Christian's heart. I was once a mother in the world of sorrow and loss. There I learned to weep, and there I also learned the priceless value of faith in God's mercy through our Lord Jesus Christ; there, Marietta, did I bid adieu to the infants, who lived but to pain a mother's heart at the parting.

Children Are Safe from Evil

"Thrice I pressed to my fond heart the loved babes, flesh of my flesh, bone of my bone and life of my life, and looking up to God, adored Him for the precious gifts. But scarcely had I with hope illumed the future, and placed my heart upon them, ere, like young and tender buds they were nipped by the frost of death, and I was left wounded and forlorn. I hoped in Jesus, and consigned them to Him, believing they were well; but, Marietta, had I only known, yea, could I have but seen what thou now seest, then would my soul have had from knowledge added to faith, greater rest, for here the babe who has left its parents in woe, but waits their arrival, and here it is safe from the contaminations of the vices and sins of the fallen race. See, Marietta," she continued, "these germs of immortality."

I beheld and lo! the interior that was opened before me was that of a temple gloriously adorned. In circular tiers, one rising above another, were niches or segments of circles. In each reposed an infant spirit. Before each was an attending or guardian angel, whose employment consists in fitting for higher life the germ formation of the spirit for its eternal existence in holy usefulness. The angel breathes upon it and every breath causes its capacity and life to expand, for the breath is that of holy love and inspiration, as her life is in God whose Quickening Spirit pervades all angels in the heavens.

As we entered, I saw that those infants, as they awoke to still greater consciousness, and as they beheld their angel bending over them, wore an expressive smile, and were happy.

Could I portray to you this one nursery, and so fix it in your mind that you could realize its glorious magnificence, then would I be more content, but I cannot.

There are also angels appointed, who touch in softest

notes, the varied instruments upon which is made melody. This music is ever mingling with that of angelic voices of sweet and heavenly utterance. So soft, sweet, and melodious was that music, that it served as life to give action and strength to the spirit nerve of those who were reposing beneath the smile of their guardians. "This," said the spirit who conducted me there, "is but one of the many of these great temples, and corresponds to all in this degree. *Here—oh! that earthly parents could realize it—is, as it were, the birth-place of those who are not permitted to tarry in the outer form until understanding awakes within them.* From this they ascend to places prepared. But, Marietta, thou hast not witnessed the most delightful of all the realities connected with this temple."

CHAPTER VII

INFANTS RECEIVED BY THE SAVIOR

As she spoke, each of the guardian angels arose with the infant of her charge, and poised in the great space around the angel who held the Cross. Instantly a light, infinitely superior to that in the temple, descended from above; and I was awed with the august presence of a retinue of angels, in whose midst was one like unto that glorious Being I had been informed was My Redeemer.

Redeemer Blesses the Children

As they approached the centre, the manifestation of the Cross disappeared before the greater light; the angel retinue paused, and the Being whom they attended smilingly said, "Suffer little children to come unto me, and forbid them not." The sweetness and gentleness of the expression, and the love that shone from his face as these words moved from his lips, overcame me, and I sank at the feet of my heavenly conductor, who raised me up, and drew me to her angel breast.

I would that the world could see and hear what then occurred. As he spoke, those guardian angels drew near, and each presented him with their treasure. He moved his hand above them, and goodness, like dew-drops, fell therefrom, and the infants appeared to drink as from a fountain of living water. They were blessed. The emanation from that Being was the breath of life. The temple wore a new aspect. As the scene was closing, the angels who attended him played upon stringed instruments, and sung of Redemption. He moved his gracious hand as if in approbation of what the guardian angels had done; and they all bowed, and veiled their faces in the garment of glory that encompassed them. Suddenly music, like the voice of many waters, arose from every temple in the broad nursery of the great city. And as the utterance

moved forth in one swelling wave of angelic song, that
Being, with those who had accompanied him, reascended,
and the angels of this temple resumed their former movement.

Earth Proper Place for Children

"This," said my guide, "is but the more simple portion of the heavenly exercises connected with the pleasing
occupation of those who are appointed to rear infant
spirits, in preparation for unfolding their being into enlarged capacity and useful employment. *The earth, if
man had not departed from purity and harmony, and
thence from affinity and companionship with beings of
an exalted nature, would have been a proper nursery for
new-born spirits.*

Moral Nature of Angels is Pure

"Sin, Marietta, removed the condition of the sinner
from that of angels; for by it his moral nature became
changed. Angels are pure. No stain is found upon them,
—no evil desires ever awaken improper energies within
them. From them emanates life in its pure element. That
life nourishes a like element. More dependent spirits arise
within their halo of divine existence. They are, in like
manner, moving within the glory that encompasses the
societies more exalted than themselves; and these are,
in like manner, moving in the light, and enjoying the
life-sphere of a still higher class of beings. Thus, all pure
spiritual beings united, exist in spheres of higher life;
and, as one being of greater capacity, exist in the life
descending from God, the Life of all. Superior orbs and
systems, in like manner, move in the spheres of those
more exalted; and, receiving perpetual supplies from
them, are refined and exalted, until the terrestrial becomes the spiritual, and the spiritual the celestial.

"The discordant are severed from the affinity of those
natures above. Men do not know the loss they sustain.

while in the darkness consequent upon their condition, and therefore they do not properly realize the necessity and benefit of a Savior. Whoever restores the affinity lost, is the Redeemer. Here those who are mature are enabled to understand the law of salvation, even life in Christ, and by means of this knowledge, are led to acceptable adoration of Him who is their Redeemer.

Heaven Filled With Praise for the Redeemer

"Thou didst notice, that as He who blessed these little ones ascended, all the nurseries of this great city chanted as one, praises to God and the Lamb. This was spontaneous; for those who know the consequences of sin are the better prepared to behold in Jesus condescension and mercy infinite, and from their inmost being, to adore him. But when he moves in their midst, they utter songs silently, which, as he is withdrawing from them, assume outward expression. These happy beings, Marietta, could no more refrain from that full manifestation of joy and thanksgiving, than life could cease to flow from Him who is the Author of Life. Thus it is throughout all heaven, and more especially all abodes of preparation for spirits of the redeemed. Dost thou not realize that each breath of those beings around thee is but a separate volume of praise to God?

"If men in the body knew the goodness of God in redemption, they would cease from evil, and learn righteousness and the ways of peace. Marietta, understandest thou this?"

I felt the reproof, knowing my former infidelity as to salvation through Jesus, and fain would have veiled my spirit from the scrutiny of that spirit who thus addressed me. I knew I had doubted the immortality of the soul, and man's restoration from evil through the Lord Jesus Christ. And now I beheld that he is all and in all; the source of every pure and holy delight, and the theme of all I had been permitted to see in the world of spirits.

Infants Blessed Now Given to Other Angels

As soon as the angels had resumed their former positions, my guide informed me, that those infant spirits I had just beheld blest by the Redeemer, had been given into the charge of other angels, whose delight was to gently train the mind by means adapted to their advancing condition; and that now was approaching a scene in which I should witness the reception of infants just from earth. As she closed, I saw above and around, angels poising in the serene atmosphere, waiting with their treasures the moment to arrive for them to enter the temple. When the former angels had given up their charge, and were preparing to receive another class, these entered and occupied the centre around the Cross.

Cause of Premature Death of Infants

"Those angels," said my guide, "encompassed in a light above that of the temple, are of a higher and more exalted nature. From them proceeds a halo of superior light. This light is the descending life of love. Dost thou not see how it concentrates, encompassing and overshadowing those germinal existences in the arms of the guardian angels? That which is nourished by each angel *is a spirit whose being is just begun, and who, by reason of nature's violated laws, has been separated prematurely from its infant form in the external world.* This soft music thrills every fibre of the being, while the Supreme Spirit is reorganizing and giving it enlarged capacity—fitting each organ to its fellow-organ in the harmony of perfection, thus establishing tone and proper energy in the system. The Quickening Spirit gives energy and expansion to the life principle unfolding, so that the intellect may perceive, the judgment operate, the understanding embrace realities, and the being enjoy the life thereof."

CHAPTER VIII

INFANTS RESTORED TO HARMONY

Again I was touched with a stream of light, by which I was enabled to discover those infants as a complex and exceedingly delicate instrument unstrung. Each separate or distinct portion had movement, but not determination; and appeared separately to lie in a sort of spasm-like action. I addressed my guide, saying, "At first I saw in the angel's arms the life-germ of an infant form. This germ was so delicate, that I could not comprehend how its guardian spirit could save the flickering taper. Then I saw descending from above a light which encompassed and pervaded the spirit. Then it moved as if receiving life and energy. Again I saw the separate tissue, apparatus, and system of organs of that infant, and lo! all were dissevered. Tell me, how shall these so varied, complicated, and deranged unite in harmony?"

Restoration of Infant Begins

Again light encompassed my spirit, and its brightness penetrated the secret chambers thereof, in which perceptions most exquisite were awakened, and a new being of my own appeared to arise and look out upon the scene. Here I saw that numberless spirit functions responded to the touch of some invisible power so that each harmonized in perfect adaptation; and as they embraced, they coalesced and were lost in identity, until I could perceive them as one; and this moved as a being distinct, full and perfect. Then each organ and function of the infant I had seen encompassed within the light of the three angels above arose, and, in like manner, corresponding to the separate organs of these, embraced each other, and so coalesced that distinction was lost; and then my soul uttered unconsciously, "Praise him for his mighty works,"

—for my spirit looked upon an infant in all the perfection of angelic life; yes, an infant restored. I had perceived it a flickering taper; then as a complex instrument unstrung; and then encompassed and pervaded by the sphere of life from the angels above. I had scanned each organ as it tremulously moved while being operated upon by the spirit of life. I had despaired of its restoration.

I now beheld that which was before dissevered from its associate, and discordant, a well-tuned instrument, in form and being an angel spirit; and as it looked up into the face of the angels, it smiled. Truly I thought here is the exposition of that text, "Marvel not that I said unto you, ye must be born again." And from what had passed before me, I felt the force of that beautiful expression of David when he said, "We are fearfully and wonderfully made." And turning to my guide, I inquired, "Is this real? Is this a spirit redeemed?"

The Restoration of a Spirit a Divine Act

"Truly," said my guide, "what thou hast seen is real. It is the unfolding to thy understanding the movement and power of grace upon the spirit that has been rendered discordant by sin, which is the violation of the law,— the law of being and the law of God. *The light descending from angels, Marietta, could not restore, and the music could not harmonize, nor could the maternal guardians supply that which was lost.* Theirs was to support the external, while this dissevering process succeeded, and the components were restored and fitted for proper use by Him who is the Redeemer, and who hath power to tune each fibre of the being, and purify and inbreathe the life of holiness into the soul, giving new life, tone, energy, inclination, and love; then to order their reunion unto perfect life in the infant form. And now thou beholdest a spirit in the consummation of the redemption.

This spirit is now prepared to rest in the soft and balmy bed of repose, whence thou hast seen others arise to higher life, Marietta, treasure this in thy soul; but learn while this has passed before thee, it is but one of all this nursery of infant life which thou hast seen.

"And now the scene changes, and another approaches. Listen, Marietta. The melody of angels moves upon the holy atmosphere of the city. They chant praises to God and the Lamb for their redemption; for great is the number of these spirits restored to the harmony of perfect beings. And thus, Marietta, are thanksgivings offered to our Heavenly Parent at each closing scene, which brings the newborn spirit into the harmony and the possession of heaven."

Oh! how my spirit caught the heavenly flame as it rose, volume succeeding volume, in ascending praise, adoration, and glory, inexpressible and divine! As said the Revelator, "It was the voice of many waters."

It appeared that the whole city resolved itself into the voice of praise. "Oh! is this heaven?" I said. How blessed it is to be accounted worthy to enter the city of God. And if this is only the Infant Paradise,—if this is the song uttered in view of the restoration to harmony and heaven of this class of infant spirits, though great their number, how vast and incomprehensible must be that expression of thanksgiving when redemption is complete, and the Bride, the Lamb's wife, shall touch the golden harp as they arise from the marriage supper, in that great day when God shall make up his jewels?

The bliss was so entrancing in its effects upon me, that I felt like ascending with the divine aspirations: but reflections upon my unfitness overcame me, and I fell into the holy arms of my guide.

CHAPTER IX

CHRIST REVEALED AS SUFFERING ON THE CROSS

As I lay in the arms of my heavenly guardian, I looked into her face, which wore an expression of deep emotion. With earnestness her eyes were fixed above; and her holy lips moved as if in prayer. At first the expression of her features was so sorrowful, that I thought she would weep; but tears would have been a feeble manifestation of that feeling which, I could plainly see, continued to increase. Truly, I said, in silent thought, do angels grieve? Can sorrow enter this Holy City? The music had ceased—its echo reverberated, and moved in the distance. Silence reigned in the vast expanse. I still leaned upon the breast of my blessed protector, anxiously observing what was passing. Light from above shone upon her brow with increasing brilliancy. Her eyes were still fixed; and, to employ earthly expressions her bosom began to heave, her lips became motionless, and her glowing countenance had the appearance of reverential awe. Her looks were so expressive, that I felt like shrinking from her arms; and was so awed, that I did not notice the cause of her excitement, until she gently, without turning her eyes, laid her hand of snowy white and spotless purity upon my head, and then removing it, raised it upward, until it pointed in the direction indicated by her fixed attention, and to my utter astonishment I there beheld the cause of her silent reverence, and the wondrous admiration which pervaded the inhabitants of the city. There—oh! that all the world but knew it!— there hung upon the Cross—and from all I could discover, bleeding and dying—my Lord and Redeemer! Oh! that sight! No human heart can know its effects upon the spirits who attend in the Infant Paradise. The crown of thorns, the nails, the mangled form, the flowing blood, the look of compassion, were so plainly manifested and combined, as to convey to the soul an idea of suffering, the most intense and excruciating.

Adoration of the Crucified One

About the Cross were congregating from every part of the city, guardian angels with their infant spirits. All, as they gathered in a circular form, manifested deep humility and holy reverence. As soon as they had assumed this uniform attitude, they held out the infant spirits whom they had in charge, directing their infant minds to the Cross and the Sacrifice. At this moment an angel descended, clothed in bright raiment, and moved around the Cross, holding in his hand his glittering crown. Then bowing he worshiped, and his worship was silent as had been that of all who congregated. After this, turning to the guardian angels he said, "Adore Him, for He is the Redeemer of a ruined race. Yea, let all Heaven adore Him!" Then as he lifted up his right hand, I saw in it a little book. In imitation all the angels in like manner raised their right hands, in each of which was also a book of like dimensions. Then appeared, as from an invisible dome, a choir of angelic beings. These had palms in their hands, and they with one voice sang praises to God and the Lamb. The first I could not understand, but they concluded saying, "Suffer children to come unto me. Of such is the kingdom. Out of the mouths of sucklings and babes Thou hast perfected praise. Amen, alleluia, amen!" Then the guardian angels drew still nearer to the Cross, presenting the spirits in their charge, while they were addressed in a manner entirely beyond my comprehension; at the close of which each infant was touched with a stream of light. They smiled and bowed their heads, while holding up in their little clasped hands the image of the Cross, which had been given them by their angels. Again they were folded in the arms of their protectors; and again the choir chanted a loud anthem, which, being echoed by the surrounding spirits, filled the city with one volume of holy melody. Then the Cross and Sacrifice disappeared, and the angels returning, whence they had come, the city was restored to its former appearance.

During this manifestation, my guide had not moved nor uttered a word, but appeared to enter into the spirit thereof, and to realize that a scene of absorbing interest had been presented.

No Heaven Without the Cross

At length I inquired, "Is there no heaven without the Cross and the Sacrifice? Each scene moves around its manifestation. Each spirit reverences it with holy awe, and each hymn of praise utters the name of the Sacrifice." She replied with suppressed accents, "The Cross is ever before the vision of redeemed spirits. In every circle is seen the Cross. Every flower, every artistic production, has the Cross, as by an invisible hand, inwrought throughout. And all instruction is based upon that blessed symbol of redeeming love, and it is the duty of the guardian angels to instruct the spirits of their charge, in the great truth of redemption, through Jesus, who suffered upon the Cross, and for this purpose each class of spirits, as they pass from their first guardian protectors, to the care of others, are in like manner congregated. And by this means the Cross and the Sacrifice are imaged and enstamped within their interior sense; and hence its nature and likeness grow into higher life and more exalted being with them. All redeemed and sanctified spirits are thus made to appear. No guile can in any way be found in them. *All angels can behold the Cross as it shines forth from the soul which has received its impress. From this cause malicious spirits or beings cannot conceal from their angels or the spirits of just men made perfect, their real nature.* Where the Cross does not shine, there is no pure love; and the heart whereon it is not visible, is not at peace with God. Marietta, in heaven there can be no guile. But this, with other manifestations, is only an introductory view of the principles represented, which in due time will be more perfectly unfolded in manifestations more specific and enlarged."

CHAPTER X

THE CITY VIEWED FROM A SUPERIOR PLAIN

Then I heard a voice from above us saying, "Come up hither." At this moment I beheld a circular expanse, like the interior of a tower, whose spiral walls formed ascending galleries, winding upward into the superior glory. This lovely pathway seemed formed of rainbows wreathed in spirals of prismatic hue, and reflecting varying but ever-beautiful tints of matchless lustre.

Borne on a cloud of essential light, that like a chariot gently ascended the spiral, we passed from the surface of the city, and advanced along the rising galleries of this tower of rainbow forms and glories. Seated by the side of my companion, the spirit who had kissed the Cross, a sense of calm composure, full of holy peace and delight far superior to any previous condition, captivated and pervaded my breast.

Marietta Views the City

Soon we emerged from the ascending gallery of rainbows and stood upon an aerial plain, resting in the transparent air above that magnificent and lofty dome which crowns the centre temple of instruction in the paradisical abode.

From this position I beheld the great city, reaching on every side beneath my view, and was so situated as to perceive at a glance the general features of its plan, and to contemplate it in its entire form as a picture of surpassing loveliness.

Beneath me the sublime Temple of Instruction, builded of most precious materials, and in a style of architecture which I am unable to describe, arose in air from the centre of a circular lawn of great extent, whose green surface appeared covered with the softest and richest verdure. Majestic trees in groups, and at regular intervals arose, bearing a profusion of fragrant and shining clusters of flowers. Beneath their shade, and on the more open spaces, appeared minute flower beds, filled with every variety of flowers and blossoming shrubs and vines. Fountains of living waters also were visible, some just rising from the green grass, and flowing through their marble channels, or through beds of golden sands, with a low and pleasant murmur; while others gushed forth in full volume to a lofty height, and descended in glowing streams of every variety of form, and were received in basins, some of which were like diamond, and others like burnished silver or the whitest pearl.

This lawn was encircled by a lofty but open trellis work; and at its eastern side appeared a gateway without doors, from the centre of which flowed forth a stream of living water, supplied from the fountains within the enclosure.

I now directed my attention to the surrounding city, and perceived that it was divided into twelve great divisions by this river of living waters, which flowing in a spiral course, was bordered on either side by a wide and regular avenue, in twelve great curves or circles, proceeding from the centre to the circumference. I also perceived that twelve other streets intersected this spiral avenue, centering in the consecrated ground about the Temple, and radiating to twelve equally divided points in the outer limit of the scene.

Sublime Architectural Arrangement of the City

As my vision followed the pathway of the flowing river and the stately avenues, my mind became absorbed till all sense of person or time was merged into the entrancing sight. The city was divided into one hundred and forty-four great wards or divisions, arranged in a series of advancing degrees of sublimity and beauty. From the outer limit to the centre was one gently ascending and encircling pathway of ever-increasing loveliness. Each building was of vast extent, and corresponded with all others as the perfect part of a most perfect whole. Thus the entire city appeared one garden of flowers; one grove of umbrage; one gallery of sculptured imagery; one undulating sea of fountains; one unbroken extent of sumptuous architecture all set in a surrounding landscape of corresponding beauty, and overarched by a sky adorned with hues of immortal light, that bathed and encircled each and every object with an ever-varying and increasing charm.

No Rivalry in Heaven

I now beheld the movement of the inhabitants. But faint is the idea that can be given, of what was moving before my sight. I can only describe it by saying, that the entire movement was melody. All the angelic multitudes appeared animated from one Inspiring Love, moving in the wisdom of one orderly plan, and having in view the unfolding of their infant charge into a condition of being which should perfectly correspond to all that visible perfection. No angel manifested a separate, personal movement, disconnected from the universal harmony, but all appeared to co-operate and to be inspired from one Superior Source. *I saw that no rivalry, emulation, or desire of selfish glory existed in the lovely groups of infants, but that each group, and the inhabitants of each nursery or palace, were united in holy affection to the superior, associate and more mature societies; and that each little child was filled with holy love, and desired to become advanced in holy wisdom and fitted to be used as an angel of light and loveliness.* I saw also, that each delighted to learn from those above, and to exercise the entire being in harmonic and unselfish works of love. In this it was revealed, that each child and each group of children advanced in orderly series, from temple to temple, from palace to palace, from circle to circle, and that as one group advanced it occupied the place just vacated by an older group and gave place to a more youthful family, in its former abode. Thus like the movement of Spring upon some unfallen Paradise, I saw each little child, as a living blossom of immortality, unfold from beauty to beauty, while all above was glory, and all around was loveliness, and all within was harmonious movement of unfolding life, love and knowledge of heaven and adoration of the Savior, and inspiration of undying joy.

Having thus beheld the City in its glory, usefulness and magnificence, my vision expanded, and beyond the extreme circle of palaces, I saw more perfectly, what I had seen before while in the City, multitudes of angels gathering around, in readiness to enter the outer temples at the appointed period. I saw that each class was congregating according to the class or school to which the infants they had with them were best adapted.

These angels approached as on wings of wind, and around them, enrobing them, was a bright cloud, which made them appear to me as if clothed with the sun. In their arms, as before stated, were infant spirits whose existence appeared to depend upon their care.

As they drew very near, each would pause a moment, poising in the holy and serene atmosphere, and then inclining to an appropriate position, would rest.

This most glorious view in its delightful unfolding was now somewhat changed, and my guide addressed me, saying, "Marietta, behold the order and glorious wonders of the first and most simple degree of a spiritual paradise. These angels thou hast seen in their employment, are ever engaged in this delightful duty. Here, as has been taught thee, infants assemble from the world whence we are; and from this blessed realm they are conducted to other and higher schools of instruction: but before thou art permitted to advance, a solemn and instructive lesson shall be given thee."

CHAPTER XI

MARIETTA DESCENDS TO REALMS OF DARKNESS

She touched my forehead again, and lo! the brightness and the glory of the scene departed, and I immediately descended, and soon was in a low and gloomy sub-
terranean vault. Darkness in thick folds encompassed me,
and a feeling of supernatural dread entered my soul and
shocked my being. A quivering and spasmodic action
wrought in fearful conflict throughout. My spirit startled
at every movement of my mind. Yea, it appeared as if
my thoughts wrestled amid the darkness. A distant roar
broke upon my ear, as if an ocean poured its mighty
waters foaming and surging down some craggy rock-
bound cataract. In vain I sought to grasp some substance
by which to impede my rapid movement, which appeared
to force me downward toward the awful abyss.

Her Vision of Hell

At this moment a blue sulphurous flash disturbed the
vault of nether darkness, and as it disappeared all around
me floated grim spectres, each enveloped in the fire of
unhallowed passion. So sudden had been the change and
so dreadful its effects upon me, that no thought but that
of horror and despair had entered my mind, until these
lurid ghosts appeared; then a more fearful terror possessed me, and I turned to seek refuge in the embrace
of my guide, and lo! I found her not! Alone and in this
dreadful place, no means are left me to express the most
faint idea of the agony of that moment. At first I thought
I would pray, but in an instant, the whole scene of my
life was before me. Then I exclaimed, "*O for one short*

*hour on earth! for space, however brief, for preparation
of soul, and to secure fitness for the world of spirits."*

The Voice of Conscience

But my conscience, as if some fiend, in a voice hoarse
and trembling, echoed, "In thy day thou didst reject and
spurn the means adapted to thy necessities, canst thou
hope for successful suit in this dark scene of woe?" And
then to add to my misery, my former doubts and skepticism arose like living beings, looking upon me with a
piercing glare. They revolved around me in condemning
mockery. Thus congregated my life's meditations. No
secret thought but now composed a part of that attending
throng; even those thoughts I had, as I supposed, forgotten, proceeded in order and strength around me.
Again they changed, and each appeared an orb revolving
in the mental, spiritual, and moral atmosphere of my being, and these, although first appearing in separate parts,
at length combined as components of myself. To escape
them was to flee from my own life. To annihilate them
would seem to blot out my own existence. Then it was
that I realized the force of the Savior's expression, "For
every idle word that man shall speak, he shall give account in the day of judgment."

The Powerlessness of False Teachings to Save

While thus my mental being seemed revolving in
outward vision about my despairing thought, and while
in the most absolute wretchedness my spirit longed to
be delivered from this nether gloom, and to repossess the
bodily form, another scene most terrible of all was suddenly made visible. It was the full and perfect representation of my Crucified Redeemer. Suddenly and in one continuous vision my entire life of thought concerning him,
passed in a separate embodiment before my mental view.

In one compartment of vision, dotted with appropriate imagery, appeared those thoughts which I had conceived of him as a man. In another compartment still, appeared a representation of my thoughts concerning his special atonement for the limited number of the elect, and there in fearful forms, appeared those thoughts which had been mine when I had conceived myself to be doomed to endless punishment, because predestined to reprobation from eternity. Still in another compartment appeared, also in forms appropriate, my thoughts concerning the eternal salvation of all mankind without the necessity of special moral reformation, and without personal and living faith in the Savior in regard to his atonement. And still in another compartment appeared, also clad in images significant of their interior nature, those thoughts concerning Salvation by morality. These separate compartments blended in one revolving sphere around me, in which were ten thousand confused and rapidly combining and separating images, which at once bewildered, excited and surcharged my mind. Thus my mental being moved in fearful vision about my thought, and every phase of doctrine concerning Christ, Heaven, Hell, Religion, or Eternal Life, which I had ever heard in discourse, or which I had conceived by study, or learned in conversation, or evolved in mental action, made a part of the tremendous sight.

Oh, how bewildering these conflicting yet associated ideas of the Redeemer! As they encircled me in one confused yet coherent cloud of imagery, I saw in each some distorted view of the Savior, but from none in their separate forms, neither in the entire cloud of changing views, could I behold him as he is, and therefore the divine glory, honor, majesty and perfection could not be manifested in their exalting and redeeming power, and I could not see him as a Prince and a Savior in that true character which he sustains to the world.

Saviour Appears Before Her

Bewildered, and ready to abandon all hope of ever escaping that abode, I had determined in my mind that the sight was the last which was to fill up the cup of woe, from which I had drank already to agony, and which to all eternity could not be drained, when lo! I saw the Savior extending his arms toward me, while from his lips in holy music fell the lovely and soul enrapturing sentence "Come unto me all ye weary and heavy laden, and I will give you rest."

How vast the contrast, when from the midst of the cloud, was revealed that glorious Being encompassed with the shining appearance of a sun. Inwrought into the revolving surface of the halo of light which encircled him, and which moved with calm but rapid motion, I beheld a representation of the true relation between the Divine Redeemer and the universe of light, where holy angels dwell, and the awful disparity between my own nature and that sphere of light and life, harmony and love.

Disharmony of Her Nature

I thus beheld him whom, in my madness, folly, and skepticism I had so often rejected. At first I wished to break from the mental embodiment which was about my inner being, and mingle the very elements of my life with this sphere of light, and to dwell in its beauty, peace, and joy: but being unable to enter into its reality by reason of the diversity existing between its exaltation and the impure elements of my fallen mind, a feeling of distrust and doubt again arose within me.

CHAPTER XII

THE ABODE OF THE LOST

Suddenly a sable veil of nether night appeared to ascend, pervading and encompassing my being. My inner doubt seemed wrought into a cloud that shut out the upper glory, and the spirit of denial plunged me into the vortex of a deeper gloom. I fell as one precipitated from some dizzy height. The embodiment of darkness opened to receive me. The moving shadow of a more desolate abyss arose like clouds in dense masses of tempestuous gloom; and as I descended, the ever-accumulating weight of darkness pressed more fearfully upon me. At length a nether plain that seemed boundless was imaged upon my sight, which, at a little distance, appeared to be covered with the sparkling semblance of vegetation. Luminous appearances, like waving trees, with resplendent foliage, and flowers and fruits of crystal and of gold, were visible in every direction.

Spirits of the Lost

Multitudes of spirits appeared beneath the umbrage, and luminous mantles were folded about rapidly moving form. Some wore crowns upon their heads; others tiaras; and others decorations of which I knew not the name, but which appeared to be wrought of clusters of jewels, wreaths of golden coin, and cloth of gold and silver tissue. Others wore towering helmets; and others circlets filled with glistening and waving plumes. A pale phosphorescence was emitted by every object, and all appeared a splendid masquerade. The apparel worn by these busy myriads corresponded with the ornaments of the head; hence every variety of sumptuous apparel was displayed upon their forms. Kings and queens appeared arrayed in the gorgeous robes of coronation. Groups of nobility of both sexes, also decorated with all the varieties of adornment displayed in the pageantry of kingly courts. Dense multitudes were visible in costume proper to the highly cultivated nations; and as they passed by, I discovered similar groups composed of less civilized tribes, attired in barbaric ornaments of every form. While some appeared clothed in the habiliments of the present day, others were in ancient attire; but every class of spirits manifested, in the midst of variety of mode, a uniformity of external pride, pomp, and rapidly moving and dazzling lustre.

A Phantom Sphere of Evil

Sounds of mingled import—bursts of laughter—utterances of revelry, of gay sport and witty ridicule, and polished sarcasm, and obscene allusions and terrible curses broke upon my ear. These again were intermixed with impure solicitations and backbitings, and hollow compliments, and feigned congratulations, and all in one sparkling brilliancy, agitated the pained, bewildered sense.

As I advanced, I walked as upon scorpions, and trod as amid living embers. The trees that seemed to wave about me were fiery exhalations, and their blossoms the sparklings and the burnings of unremitting flames. Each object I approached by contact created agony.

Realm of Illusion

The phosphorescent glare that surrounded the various objects burned the eye that looked upon them. The fruitage burned the hand that plucked and the lips that received it. The gathered flowers had emitted a burning exhalation, whose fetid and noisome odor, inhaled in the nostrils, caused excruciating pain. The fiery atoms of the atmosphere burned as they were wafted by me. The air and the blast that moved it, alike were burdened with the very elements of disappointment and wretchedness.

Upon turning to see if I could discover a single drop of water to allay the fierce and intolerable thirst; fountains appeared, and rivulets flowed amid the herbage, and lay in calm and placid pools. Soon, however, I discovered that these corresponded with the former illusions, and the drops of spray from the sparkling fountains fell like drops of molten lead upon the shrinking form. The flowing rivulets were like the molten river of metallic fire that streams from a furnace seven times heated; and the deep still pools were as the white and waveless silver in some glowing crucible, when every atom is burning with a fierce, intolerable glow.

A Lost Spirit Speaks

When in solemn contemplation of these fearful scenes, a spirit approached me whom I had known on earth. This being appeared externally far more brilliant than when in the body. The form, the countenance, the eyes, the hands, appeared endued with a metallic lustre that varied with every motion and every thought. Accosting me the spirit said:

"Marietta, we are again met. You see me a disembodied spirit, in that abode where those who inwardly deny the Savior find their habitation when their mortal day has ended.

"Strange emotions agitate your bosom. Thus I felt, looked, wondered, and moved in sad and bewildered anxiety in the hour when my being here discovered the theatre of its present existence. But I experienced that which you have never yet realized in the interior principles of mind. Strange and incontrollable are the emotions causing me to relate that inward sorrow which this brilliant exterior would, if it were possible, conceal.

The Wicked Go to Their Own Place

"My life on earth was suddenly brought to a close; *and as I departed from the world, I moved rapidly in the direction prompted by my ruling desires.* I inwardly desired to be courted, honored, admired—to receive universal adulation, and to be free to follow the perverted inclinations of my proud, rebellious, and pleasure-loving heart—a state of existence where all should be pleasure without restraint—where each should be free to obey the promptings of every passion, and where every indulgence should be permitted to the soul,—where prayers and religious instructions should find no place—where the Sabbath should not be known—where no rebuke of sin should ever fall—where existence should be spent in gay and festive sports, with no superior and restraining power to molest or interfere.

"With these desires I entered the spirit world, and passed to the condition adapted to my inward state. I rushed in haste to the enjoyment of the glittering scenes which you now behold. I was welcomed as you have not been, for at once I was recognized as a fit associate by those who here abide. They do not welcome you, for they discern in you an interior desire, adverse to the ruling passions which here prevail.

A Welcome in Hell

"I was welcomed with gay and sportive sounds. The beings whom you behold in the distance rushed forward to embrace me. They shouted, 'Welcome! Welcome!' I was awed, bewildered, and yet mentally quickened and energized by the atmosphere of this abode. I found myself endued with the power of strange and restless motion.

"Every organ sent forth and every pore emitted a phosphorescent illumination, which condensed about the head and formed the appearance of a brilliant diadem.

and reflected on the countenance a wild, unearthly glow. The exhalation as it extended became a flaming robe, enveloping my form and causing it to conform in appearance to the invariable likeness of my spirit associates.

"I became conscious of a strange pervasion of the brain, and the cerebral organs became subject to a foreign power, which seemed to operate by an absolute possession.

Hell's Revelry Palls but Does Not Appease

"I abandoned myself to the attractive influences that were around me, and sought to satisfy my craving desires for pleasure. I reveled, I banqueted, I mingled in the wild and voluptuous dance, I plucked the shining fruit, I plunged in the ardent streams, I surfeited my nature with that which externally appeared delicious and inviting to the sight and to the sense. But when tasted, all was loathing and a source of increasing pain. And so unnatural are the desires perpetuated here that what I crave I loathe, and that which delights tortures me. My tortures create within me a strange intoxication. My appetite is palled, and yet my hunger is unappeased and unappeasable.

"Every object which I perceive I crave, and I grasp it in the midst of disappointment and gather it with increased agony. With every new accession of experience I am immersed in some unknown fantasy, delirium and intoxication. New and strange phenomena are continually manifested and add delirium to delirium, and fear to fear. I seem to myself to become part of that which is about me. The voices which fall upon my ear, again burst from me in incontrollable utterances. I laugh, philosophize, jeer, blaspheme and ridicule by turns, yet every epithet, however impure, sparkles with wit, glows with metaphor, and moves adorned with every rhetorical embellishment. The metallic ores, the waving trees, the shining fruit, the moving phantasms, the deluding waters, seem to form a dazzling and mocking spectacle, which is ever before my eyes, and every subject of reflection, has its fellow in my heart, from which, in its mocking scenery, it meets a response. I inwardly crave to satisfy my hunger and my thirst, and the desire appears to create without and around me a tantalizing illusion of cool waters I may never drink, and grateful fruits I may never taste, and refreshing airs I never feel, and peaceful slumbers I may never enjoy. I know that the forms around me are fantastic and delusive, yet every object appears to hold controlling power, and to domineer with cruel enchantment over my bewildered mind.

The Law of Evil Attraction

"I experience the power of the law of evil attraction. I am the slave of discordant and deceptive elements and of their presiding vice. Every object by turns attracts me. The thought of mental freedom dies within the dying will, while the idea that I am a part and an element of the revolving fantasy takes possession of my spirit.

"This realm, curtained with a cloud of nether night, is one sea of perverted and diseased magnetic element. Here lust, pride, hate, avarice, love of self, ambition, contention, and blasphemies, reveling in madness, kindle into a burning flame. And that speciality of evil which does not belong to and unfold from one spirit, belongs to and unfolds from another; so that the combined strength of the aggregate of all, is the prevailing law. By this strength of evil I am bound, and in it I exist.

"Here are those who oppressed the poor; who robbed the hireling of his wages, and bound the weary down with heavy burdens; the false in religious faith; the hypocrite; the adulterer; the assassin; and the suicide, who, not satisfied with life in the external form, has hastened its close.

The Folly of the Suicide

"Did mortals but know the dark and dreadful night into which they are sure to fall if they die unprepared, they would desire to lengthen the day of probation rather than to hasten its termination, however multiplied their scenes of sorrow, and to wisely improve the fleeting moments which quickly number earth's probationary scenes. Is man's weary existence fraught with grief while he walks the gloomy dells of death, and gropes along the brambly paths that mortals tread? Here, on either hand, awake new and multiplied causes of accumulating gloom. Does hope of peaceful and happy days in the outer world flicker like the dying taper? In this abode are ceaseless, unsatisfied, and unholy inclinations.

"Here also sense is infinitely more acute. What with mortals would produce only a pang, enters into the very elements of our existence, and the pain becomes a part of us. And as immortality is the intellectual sensation of man unincumbered with physical sense, and vastly superior in its ability to endure to mortality, in like proportion is the consciousness and capability of suffering here, superior to human suffering.

The Result of the Violated Law

"Marietta, I feel 'tis vain to attempt the expression of our deplorable state. I often inquire, is there no hope? And my sense replies, How can harmony exist in the very midst of discord? We were advised of the consquences of our course while in the body; but we loved our ways better than those which exalted the soul. We have fallen into this fearful abode. We have originated our sorrow. God is just. He is good. We know that 'tis not from a vindictive law of our Creator that we suffer. Marietta, it is our condition from which we receive the misery we endure. The violation of the moral law, by which our moral natures should have been preserved in harmony and health, is the prime cause of our state. O sin! thou parent of countless woes! thou insidious enemy of peace and heaven! why do mortals love thy ways?"

Here she paused and fixed her eyes, wild with despair, upon me. I shrank from the dreadful glare, for the appearance manifested inexpressible torture.

While she was addressing me, a multitude of the forlorn beings were moving around her, striving to suppress their true feelings, while listening to her relation of the reality of their sufferings. Their appearance, her address and the scene which was before me, filled me with horror; and I sought to escape. Upon discovering this, her grief appeared to deepen, and she hastily said:

"No, Marietta, leave me not, can you not endure for a short period the sight and relation of what I am continually suffering? Tarry with me, for I desire to speak many things.

Land of Hoplessness

"Do you startle at these scenes? Know then that all that moves around you is but the outer degree of deeper woe. Marietta, no good and happy beings abide with us. All within is dark. We sometimes dare to hope for redemption, still remembering the story of Redeeming Love, and inquire, Can that love penetrate this abode of gloom and death? May we ever hope to be made free from those desires and inclinations which bind us like chains, and passions which burn like consuming fires in the unhallowed elements of this world of wretchedness?"

Overcome by her deep feelings, she yielded to the manifestation of grief, and I heard her speak no more; whereupon another spirit drew near, and addressing me, said:

Memory of Lost Opportunity

"Go, leave us to our lot. Your presence gives us pain, since it revives the more active memory of lost opportunities; the indulgence of propensities that folded around the soul the elements of evil magnetism, and pervaded the spirit with its deadly miasm."

Here the spirit paused a moment, then continued, "No, tarry; prompted by a cause I know not, I am desirous to reveal what we have learned while here, relative to the power and influence of evil and its magnetism upon the spirit of man, which, though while man inhabits the tenement of clay is exceedingly subtile, when the spirit leaves the outer world and enters the interior world, forms the external sphere of his existence. Here it is the more external. In the world whence we came, it is the invisible and interior; but now it is our outward dwelling. It arises from the deep. It unfolds from the soul. It encompasses all, pervades all, controls and inspires all. Mortals are opposed to this truth, and from the love and goodness of God, they reason that there can not be suffering in the spirit of man. This reasoning charges evil upon God, since evil and suffering exist with the family of man in the outer world and with us prevail. The cause of this is obvious, and yet men seek to reject the principle.

The Harvest of Sin

"When the harmony and movement of law is disturbed or prevented, evil consequences ensue. Man, by counteracting the movement of law in himself, produces a contrary effect from what is indicated, and therefore, that which was ordained unto life—that which should have perfected him—by improper tendencies, is operative unto death; sin therefore, or the violation of law, unfits the being for proper development, and hence, the violator being removed from harmony, dies unto (ceases to exist in) the law of peace and holy development.

"This great and irrevocable truth is manifest in every degree of physical and moral movement, where law meets with obstruction; and we have its fruits with us in abundant and fearful harvest.

Remorse Too Late

"Why will not mortals reason and discover the results of action, and by preventing the growth of evil and by cleaving unto God, through heaven appointed means, escape these fearful consequences? Marietta, you are not one of us, else these elements would have envelopd your being and absorbed your life. But you will return to realms of peace. Madness and delirium arise and rage within us upon being cited to scenes where love, pure love, and peace abide. You are thus addressed because of your return to earth. Tell the inhabitants thereof what you have seen, and warn them of the danger awaiting those who persist in the gratification of impure desires."

Recognition in Hell

One hideous expression closed the scene; and being overcome—for I knew what I had witnessed was real— I was immediately removed. *Those spirits I had known on Earth, and when I saw them there I knew them still.* Oh, how changed! They were the very embodiment of sorrow and remorse. How ardently I desired that they might escape and become pure, and receive an inheritance with those blessed spirits I visited in Paradise of Peace.

CHAPTER XIII

THE ABYSS—REALM OF THE DESPERATELY WICKED

During these reflections I unconsciously passed away from that sphere of gloom to a region where I could perceive nothing but lonely space. No sun or stars were visible to my sight. Darkness more dense, close around me, and I felt that my doom was sealed, and that I should soon become the companion of spirits in those fantastic realms. And when I began to agonize beneath the idea of departing hope, I heard a voice as from the distance, in tones soft and melodious, say, "Look unto Jesus: He is the life of the soul." In a moment an inward feeling arose in rebellion to the idea of adoring that Jesus who was crucified; when suddenly all that seemed to sustain me departed, *and again I descended as from an immeasurable height, into an abyss inhabited by beings, whose condition I did not at first discover, but who were finally revealed as more desperate than those from whom I had just escaped.* They gathered around me and commended me for the doubt I had entertained concerning the Divinity of the Son of God. Then a spirit of giant intellect, approaching me, said:

Address of the False Philosopher

"Religion, the Religion of the Bible, so much revered by many who live in darkness and are undeveloped, is but a spiritual farce. The God of the Bible whom Christians call Savior of the World, was but a man. Religious faith circumscribes the range of human thought, fetters the noble intellect, and prevents the progression of the race. Those thou hast just visited, are a class of spirits who, blinded by the delusive dreams of Earth's religionists, have entered the spirit world unprogressed; hence they still cling to the idea of Redemption through Christ. They appear to suffer; their suffering is but imaginary. Light will ere long reach them. Then will they be enabled to discover the folly of their religious education, to which, though discarded by their better being, they cleave with insatiable desires. We are free. Our intellect ranges unrestrained, and we behold the magnificence and the glory of the peopled universe. We enjoy the rich productions of the sublime attributes of mind, and thus—and not by the Religion of the Cross—we arise into the more exalted spheres of intellectual attainments, and the moving grandeur of terrestrial things.

"Marietta, for so thou art called, we saw thee when darkness overshadowed thee, and well did we understand that for a moment, from the force of education, thou wouldst have offered prayer for salvation in the name of Jesus. We heard that voice that spake from above thee, saying, 'Look to Jesus'; still that did not save thee. Learn, then, that from the native unfolding of thy being cometh salvation.

Free Thinkers in Hell

"What dost thou see, Marietta? Abandon thy thoughts of the empty Religion of the Bible, and behold the wonders of this sphere of existence. This is the Second Sphere. Around thee gather minds from the varied spheres of Earth, minds whose strength of intellect could not yield to the force of an imaginary religion. They were not awed into reverence by the priestly garb, nor sang the idle notes of psalmody, the heartless 'music' of the church.

"These sing of nature, of which they are a noble part; and thus united, ascend the octave of mental progressive harmony."

Here the spirit addressing me became greatly annoyed;

and the nebulous appearance which encompassed him was agitated under the influence of successive shocks, which caused his very being to convulse and writhe beneath its influence. I could not perceive whence they came, and was greatly terrified, as I saw the whole scene changed at every successive touch, which was attended with flashes like broad sheets of lurid light, playing upon the cloud-like form which enveloped him.

Exposure of the False Philosophy

I could also perceive that he was intensely struggling to overcome some power which was about to control him. Every energy was exerted to its highest capacity, to roll back the tide that was overwhelming him. Suddenly he groaned, as in the bitterness of one sinking to irremiadable despair, and then yielded to the intrusive influence, when, lo! a vast arena opened to my view, in which I saw at one glance every imaginable species of vice, forms and fashions of human society, government, clans, and all the varied phases and forms of worship, originating in every kind of religion, from the heathen to fashionable church-going people, who heartlessly worship under the name of the holy Religion of the Cross.

The Pandemonium—Mock Worship

As this scene opened, I heard a voice from far above me, saying, "Marietta, fear not; but behold a pandemonium, where congregate the self-deceived; hopers in false philosophy, together with the despisers of God; and where also arise, in spectral form, the false religions of Earth; where hypocrisy unveils its hideous shape, and religious mockery speaks in its own language; where are exhibited human wolves, who appeared in sheep's clothing, that they might indulge their cupidity upon the humble and unsuspecting. Hark! listen to that wild chant which breaks from the thousands who sit in the galleries of song. They once sung—heartlessly sung—

hymns dedicated to the worship of the living God. Listen to the hoarse voice of the heavy organ before which they are congregated. See, they arise; observe their manner, and seek to understand what they utter."

As I approach the description of this scene, I most sensibly feel my incompetency. The reality none can ever know, save those who personally behold it. I am only able to say, that every evil device which prevails with man, appeared organized and moving in a perfect scene, and each spirit was an actor performing the part cultivated by him while in the body. I knew that if they expected bliss, all was unreal; and yet all struggled to obtain enjoyment, which, however, from its dreadful fantasy, recoiled upon the suffering soul with inexpressible horror.

The False Priest

As I looked upon them, the occupants of the broad galleries arose; and as they sung, the hoarse voice of the spectral organ jarred, as note after note of their attempted music fell from lips whose very accents mocked the effort. My soul pitied them, as I saw them sink back in utter despair; and yet I thought I could perceive design in their movements. Below them were seated a fastidious audience, before whom was standing, in a pulpit of Gothic architecture, one clad in priestly garb—one who had dishonored the cause of the Redeemer by hypocrisy and the love of vain glory—who had made the cause of the holy ministry a by-word, by a soulless profession of love for the gifts of grace. This representation of speculators in religious things, moved in the mock dignity of his clerical profession. Before him lay an open volume, from which he attempted to read, but every effort was baffled. His voice was shrill and piercing, and his accents inarticulate. His features became distorted, and he writhed and agonized. He then attempted to read again, which resulted as did the first, increasing his sufferings, until he burst forth in the most vehement expressions, cursing his own being, and all around him, and then blasphemously addressing himself to the Author of Existence, charged God with all wrong, the source of every sorrow, and even desired to gather together the strength of all created intellect with which to curse the Creator of the Universe. His oaths, his manner, and his insatiable passion, caused him to appear so desperate, that I felt impressed with fear that he had power to accomplish great destruction in whatever direction he moved.

Soon, however, my anxiety was relieved by the sudden exhaustion of his entire force, and I saw that he too, was limited in power, and was, moreover, to a very great extent, under the will of his audience.

One glance at the throng before him, was sufficient to reveal the cause of much of his suffering. There, were seated those who countenances bespoke interior hate, mingling with wild maniacal relish; those who mocked his futile effort and indulged in fiendish delight at the expense of his dreadful sufferings. Yea, they relished his manifestation of keen despair as the uneasy wound relishes that friction which affords present maddening pleasures, but terminates in more excited pain. As he sank back, the expression of his countenance was that of horror beyond description. His being assumed every imaginable distortion. Around him flashed lurid fires, and his entire outward expression, revealed an inward consciousness as restless as some burning crater. His whole appearance bespoke agonies equal to the worst conceptions of the relentless sinner's hell, and reminded me of the language of Jesus, who said, "And they shall go into outer darkness, where there shall be weeping and wailing and gnashing of teeth; where the worm dieth not and the fire is not quenched." While he lay enveloped in the fires of his own unhallowed passions, one of his audience arose and thus addressed him:

Condemnation of the Hypocrite

"Thou fiend of darkness! thou child of hypocrisy! deceiver, matchless deceiver! thine is the hell of a heartless religious teacher. Adequate sufferings thou canst never endure. Thou madest merchandise of religion and the souls of men. Yea, because of this, thou didst dwell in temples of human glory, receiving the adoration of men; then thou didst wrap thyself in the garments of ease at the expense of souls; thou didst not seek to reach the ruined heart with the soul-redeeming Truth of Heaven, but to please the ear and charm the fancy. Now thou art tormented. Arise! thou false teacher, arise! and in thy silken gown display the order of thy false apostleship. Speak to us smooth things. Direct the movement of this broad gallery of mimic song. Hold thy blasphemy! vent not thy cursings, for lo! thy Maker is just; wish not to move him from his throne. His august majesty thou didst mock. Through thee, his glory should have shown, and by that light thousands should have been led to seek his face."

At this sharp rebuke the sufferer sought to escape, whereupon the speaker continued,

"Nay, thou hypocrite! even though thou wouldst thou canst not flee. Cast thy vision over this vast throng of sufferers, then ask thyself the cause. Though these have sinned, and each to his Master standeth or falleth, canst thou behold them in peace and a sense of innocence? Didst thou strive to lead them up to God? Yea, rather thy learned essays and elaborate expositions of the Sacred Word, adorned with poetic genius, addressed with most eloquent display, did they not lull in deeper slumber the dormant spirit, while wreathing thy mortal brow with human laurels?"

Despair of the Wicked Priest

Here the spirit addressed cried out, "Hold! hold!

spare me! I suffer the tortures of unabating remorse! Dread retribution! stay! oh, stay! nor cut thy victim down. I own my sufferings just. In life I sought the means of human pleasure. I trifled with the souls of men, and heartlessly wrote of eternal things. I formed my prayers for human hearing, and interpreted the Sacred Text to gratify the capricious, the selfish, the vaunter in holy things, the usurper of human rights, the oppressor. Horror, the horrors of immortal night and keen remorse take hold of my spirit. I hear the voice of lamentation. I see the madness of disappointed spirits. These haunt me. If I seek to fly, before me congregate like ghosts the was administered by thee, our religious teacher. The multitude of ills hanging upon the soul that here finds no rest. These, my parishioners, drive me mad with their bitter imprecations. Secret sins, like demons commissioned to inflict on me immortal pain, arise from the vault of memory. Spare me a deeper hell!'!" During these ejaculations the whole audience arose and mocked his agony. At the close, the spirit addressing him resumed his animadversion, saying:

Bitter Incriminations in Hell

"Well didst thou know our delight was to please thee; and when we indulged in the gratification of desires unhallowed, and leading in the ways of death, no reproof Bible—oh! that sacred Book, gift of God to guide the wanderer to bright mansions in heaven—was made, by the false interpretations of the pleasure-loving and heartless divine, the passport to this scene of woe, where sins ripen into living forms, where fashions, with their gaudy folds, enwrap the spirit as with innumerable sheets of inextinguishable fire, and where Mammon, like a spectral goddess, sits in the clouds of death, which encanopy the abyss.

"The law of being, inverted, culminates in the fan-

tasy in which thou art moving. This thou hast done,
urged on by the love of glory, the glory of the hypocrite,
whose form of religion is like a whited sepulchre, to the
outward view fair as the spotless Church, which reflects
the glory of the Spiritual Jerusalem from bright worlds
on high. But thy heart was the seat of pride and lust, a
cage of foul birds, a den of reptile thoughts. Yes, a sepulchre full of dead men's bones, the anatomic fragments of
departed, heartless divines, the legacy of religious bigots.

The Wages of Sin

"Curse not thy Maker. This is thy harvest. Listen to
that scripture so often carelessly falling from thy lips.
'He that soweth to the flesh shall of the flesh reap
corruption.' 'The wages of sin is death.' How those
passages of Holy Writ ring through the brassy chambers
of souls congregated in the realms of night. Yes, they
ring as from spirit to spirit they move, touching each
immortal sensation drawn to its highest tension by the
horror of the doom and the phantom scenes that arise
like ghosts from beneath these spheres of death.

"No, false teacher, let God be true; for sin hath formed us thus. We suffer the consequences of violated law,
the law of our being."

As he spoke these words, a fearful trembling seized
his form. He became more and more agitated, until he,
with the great congregation, quaked and fell like dead
men; and losing identity, presented one vast body of
agitated life. Above this body arose a thick atmosphere
of moving atoms, so dense, that it appeared like a part
of the mass below.

Mercy Spurned

The sight was too much; and being unable to endure
further these scenes of woe, I shrank back and exclaimed,
"Is there not a God of mercy, and can he behold and not
save?"

"Yes," spake a voice from above me, "yes there is a God of mercy, and that God beholds with pitying eyes the sinner. Mercy yearns over him. Yea, hast thou not read, 'God so loved the world, that he gave his only-begotten Son, that whosoever believeth in him should not perish, but have eternal life?' But though salvation is offered to the world, and Heaven's messengers plead with the sinner, millions refuse, and millions more who profess, speculate upon the great truth connected with man's redemption. Sin indulged, forms the sinner for woe; and there are many who will not forsake their evil ways until fallen into the most wretched state, the consequence of the violation of the law of purity and love.

The Consequences of Sin

"Fear not, Marietta, before thee has been portrayed a portion of the consequences of sin upon the spirit of man. Spiritual sufferings are beyond any power of expression; nor may they be perfectly mirrored upon the understanding by figures of representations. He who first addressed thee, represents that spirit of antichrist which seeks to dazzle spiritual perception by bright pictures of false reasoning, behind all of which lies the scene of discord, improper affections, impure desires, love of self, false hearts, cruelty, lust, rapine, and murder; the denial of God in his redeeming mercy, sacrilege and blasphemy. He strove to direct thy attention to an opposite scene, and thereby conceal the state of those whose hearts are not controlled by the love of God.

"His power failing, represents the utter futility of all things out of Christ, to save the soul from the influences tending to death which, through sin, infect the unregenerate heart.

"Then opened a scene in which was likewise portrayed all forms of vice; but too heavily would that view have borne upon thee, had it been displayed in its fulness, hence immediately appeared the gallery of choralists. These represent the world making melody to the gods of their worship, of whatever name or character they chanced to be. In their hearts was no fear or love for the Supreme Being, whom they mocked with lip service. In the desk was represented a false teacher, and the awful consequences of hypocrisy in religion. He was false, and therefore fallen into this pit of woe. Before him were those who represent the worshipers in the name of the Cross, but who have not the fear of God before their eyes. They appeared unto men to worship, but their hearts were far from God. They sought to please themselves in their devotions, while they chose a teacher who in turn sought to glorify himself with men by gratifying the caprice of his audience.

"He strove to address them in representation of the great truth, that the mind works out in the spirit, the cultivation and impression received in the outer world. His ineffectual effort represents the inability of any being to derive real satisfaction, or to be useful to those around him by false methods.

"The spirit addressing him, represents the spirit of those who, in any sphere of existence, had trusted to false teachers, and had little concern for their spiritual interests. And thus the discordance of beings not properly united is made to appear. They charge their sins upon each other. The spirit's reference to the justice of their condition as a natural consequence following the violation of law, represents the consciousness of guilt and the goodness of God, conceived by all who awake from their idle dreamings to a proper sense of the requisition of God's holy law upon them.

Like Attracts Like

"The dreadful writhing of the spirit addressed under the dark picture of his past deeds, represents that those who, in external life follow their carnal desires, when they meet in spirit reflect great truths upon each other, by the thoughts and movements of their being. Their final fall and blending into one, illustrates the inseparable nature and tendency of sin; also, that the law of sympathy or magnetic affinity, exists even with the disembodied spirits of men; and that, by that law, like character of mind and affections, are attracted to each other, and that by accumulation, prevailing elements increase in power and momentum, and thus each receives from and inflicts sorrow upon the other.

"The moving cloud above them also illustrates the atmosphere of thought which fills the great arena of spiritual discord.

"Finally, Marietta, the scene of the bishop and his congregation, together with the false teachers of the schools of vain philosophy, illustrates that portion of the sacred text which saith, 'If the blind lead the blind, both shall fall together.'

"Marietta, thy spirit cannot endure more; but let this lesson impress thee with the great truth, that 'the wages of sin is death.' "

CHAPTER XIV

MARIETTA ASCENDS FROM THE ABYSS

As the voice addressing me ceased, I heard an angel from some choral band, say, "Marietta, come up hither!" and I arose into a cloud of light, which gently ascended. In its pavilion my spirit rested.

The change how great, how marvelous! A moment before I was with fear and wonder beholding an excited, suffering throng reveling in the madness of inflamed passions: passions cultivated while in the body to excessive indulgence. There, they had sorrow. There, were manifested, undisguised, the effects of evil of every character, of demoralizing habits, secret purposes, and hidden iniquity. There were contentions, murmurings, and dreadful blasphemies, while the actors and sufferers were drawn together and held by prevailing elements, the elements of their own perverted natures.

Sin Works Death

And from their condition I had learned that sin worked death, and happiness cometh not by disobedience, but by unsophisticated faith: faith in Jesus as the Redeemer which incites the true worship of God from a broken heart and contrite spirit. Moreover, I also learned, that deceit was the element of darkness and the source of many woes, as well as the covert for the concealment of the end of falsehood and the fruits of vice. And yet was plainly revealed the great truth that no deception however finely wrought, can shroud in the hour of trial; for he who essayed to portray the glories of nature, and sought by the display of the emblazoned canopy to allure the soul from the Cross, and proffer life and peace by other means, failed to conceal the drama moving in the

broad arena where congregate those who do not love
God or regard his law—despisers of the holy religion of
Jesus by which men are saved.

Heaven for the Willing

I was reflecting upon this scene when new light broke
in upon me. I turned to see whence it issued, when,
lo! above me, I saw a lovely being, clad in raiment bright
as the sun, reposing in the glory surrounding her. Her
countenance shone with heavenly goodness. Calmly she
dwelt in the midst of the divine effulgence. She spake,
and her voice filled me with delight, saying, "Rest spirit,
rest. Let no care depress thee. Dismiss thy thoughts upon
the scenes just passed. *For every willing heart God hath
in heaven a mansion prepared. And whoso seeks shall
find the Lord a present help in time of need. Those thou
hast seen are in the element they indulged while in the
body. As he who falls from some dizzy height must bear
the pain the wound imparts, even so he who lives and dies
in sin, receives the counterpart. This is the law of being.*

"Rest, Marietta, rest; for lo! angelic bands descend.
List, sister. That harmony, how sweet! How gently it
moves along the heavenly way! It nears us, Marietta; the
volume swells upon the heavenly breeze. Its notes accent
praises to our Redeemer. Heavenly anthems awake on
every hand. Look up, Marietta; lo! we are near a city
wherein dwelleth righteousness. No evil enters there. No
false spirit shall ever pollute the holy temples thereof.
Hark, sister spirit, an angel guardian of the holy hills,
addresseth thee."

The Attractive Power of Evil

Then there came a voice saying, "Marietta, whence
art thou? Hast thou left the world of mortal sadness?
And why art thou inclined to scenes where evil passions

reign? Does thy being vascillate between the spheres of good and evil? I have seen thee in the Paradise of Peace, moving with the blessed, where songs unite and anthems are ever ascending in softest melody. I have seen thee floating in the murky air friendless and alone: thence I witnessed thy sudden fall into the cloud that o'erhangs the arena of inharmonious, wicked beings; and then I saw thee observing every movement until the sight overcame thee; and sinking beneath the burdened vision. I heard thee call for help from God or for some kind angel to befriend thee. Learn from this, that he whose heart is not established in truth, whose nature is not controlled by the law of holy love, is exposed to the attracting influence of evil; for there is no safety for the soul not born of Divine Good. He who hath not this principle, is in moral condition exposed to those influences which tend to outer darkness, and the abode of those existing in the sphere of deadly magnetism. *Remember that he who would be the disciple of Truth and enter into rest, must deny himself the gratification of the unholy inclinations of the perverted heart, which cleave to that which does not inspire reverence for God or a desire to be found doing His will;* and he must convert the attributes of his being to the exercise of welldoing, for thus and thus only can be secured through grace divine, everlasting good.

"Marietta, these scenes and the opening of thy spiritual perceptions are permitted for a wise purpose. *The movement of human minds, unsettled in religious truth, thou hast represented when attracted to paradise, thence to vacant regions where Chaos and Night rule chief monarchs; and thence to scenes of wretchedness where are those whose characters have been formed by wrong indulged, and the love thereof cherished, until the receptive powers have become drunken with the excess of vice, and delirious under the influence of hallucinating pleasures. And where at last the elements of evil operate un-*

controlled, and the soul made sensible of the nature of false influence, realizes the tendency and the effects of sin.

"Thus it is revealed, that when left to itself, the perverted spirit drives madly on under the insatiable action of evil, and by association devoid of restraint, spirits aggravate each other's woe; and therefore those in the broad arena were mutual sufferers.

"So also in the world of mortality, sin is strengthened in proportion to the number of minds actuated by its principles. Thus one evil doer supports another in the ways of evil. And herein is seen how one sinner destroyeth much good. Sin added to sin enlargeth its capacity, and increaseth its movement, until families, tribes and nations arm themselves to do battle in its behalf. O, that mortals but knew the power of evil influence! Then prompted by the law of heavenly love, the Spirit of Grace, they would unite to prevent its workings in the carnal heart. Marietta, woe may well be written upon the dome encompassing the race of man, *for by their indulgence in sin they embitter their mortal existence, and too often enter the world of spirits preponderating to evil, and thence become united to those existing where like elements prevail.* But the grace of God if admitted into the understanding and affections, changes the character and inclinations; since Divine Life descending into the soul, causes the affections thereof to incline to its source. And such when they enter here, by the law of holy attraction, mingle in life's sunstaining sphere, and from God receive the inspiration of holiness, the ever increasing spirit of divine attainments."

Center Dome of Infant Paradise

"Marietta, this is the city where thou hast beheld the infant nurseries, to which, from scenes of sorrow and death thou art permitted to return. From this position above the center dome of the infant nursery, thou canst behold the order and use of this temple of education. Here are congregated the schools of Infant Paradise, and here they are instructed in the higher degrees of useful employment."

As the spirit closed, suddenly the great dome below us opened, and presented at one single view its glory and magnificence. In it I saw united all the grandeur, variety and order of the entire paradise. Again, I saw in the center, the Cross. Around it were twelve spirits, in each of whose hands was a lesser cross and a harp. Each infant appeared to expect directions from the twelve spirits who were around the cross, upon whom they now fixed their attention. O, how blissful the silence that prevailed and which revealed the perfect order and Divine harmony of the place.

CHAPTER XV

MARIETTA LEARNS OF HER UNFITNESS TO ENJOY HEAVEN

"Listen, Marietta," said the angel; and with her right hand she pressed my temples, and lo! from that deep silence came forth music like the angelic breath, of the most inward and hallowed life of the spirit. I could scarcely hear it; still in softest melody it moved over the octavian organism of my inward being. Until then I had not known that within me were elements which could be awakened to such symphony; or if tuned, could vibrate to the touch of such sacred and interior melody.

Human Nature Discordant With Harmony of Paradise

As the notes of that spirit of music arose, I thought a new nature was given me to enable me to realize harmony so perfect; and I seemed to blend with it, until my own volition sought to unite, and then—oh! then— I felt the effects of a soul unstrung. Note after note from the invisible source approached this inward life of mine, but no more moved in unison with the music chords of my being; since in striving to blend in the movement they produced discord, and the several cadences were by it repelled and broken like the fall of smooth waters upon some rocky and uneven surface. The music became harsh to me, in that I knew my unlikeness to its nature. Then I suffered. Oh! the agony of that moment. The contrast was dreadful. Every part of my being was out of order. The waves of harmony that moved softly and gently throughout the dome, fell like disturbed waters into my unfitted and discordant heart. I fain would have escaped, for any other condition would be preferable by far. I thought even the arena of mimic worship would better comport with my nature, and there I could more easily harmonize with the prevailing law. But I could not escape. I was a perfect wreck; and each moment rendered my condition more awful, until an hour would appear an age. At length I cried in the bitterness of my soul, "Away; oh! let me fly from this scene. Other music has filled me with delight—other melody rendered me happy. To it I listened; and while I heard I drank in the spirit of the sacred song. But now, by some unknown law, I am prompted to attempt union with this harmonious sweetness, and lo! I am in my unhallowed nature discovered. All are witnesses of my discordance; and to myself I now appear unfit for angelic association, and lost beyond redemption. My spirit is wounded, broken, fallen; no part thereof is adapted to its fellow. Oh! let me fly away where darkness, with her sable pall, may hide me for ever from myself. Angel, veil, oh! veil this light that discovers my deformity, and save me from the torments of this angelic harmony. Oh! is there a deeper hell? Should demons mock around the lost spirit, there would be nothing to awaken this new life, or by calling into action the unstrung spiritual being, crush it with a sense of its unfitness; and no other power but this interior harmony can touch the spirit's most conscious element, and break up the hidden fountains of the unstrung and unsanctified soul."

Marietta Learns Why an Unsanctified Soul Is Unfit for Heaven

Thus I plead to be released by some method, from the light, the harmony, and the bliss that filled to the utmost capacity of enjoyment, the great congregation. My suffering was beyond expression, and yet at the time I did not consider the cause any farther than the fact that my soul was unstrung. I realized my entire unfitness for the employment, the society, and the happiness of the members of that paradise. On former occasions I had desired to be admitted with them, and to ever abide in that holy sanctuary, but had not properly considered what qualifications were wanting in me, in order that I could join them in their holy anthems. True, I had witnessed the deformity of the infant spirit, and had with wonder beheld the operations of Grace in its restoration; but never had I understandingly applied this knowledge to myself.

Hell Is Better Than Heaven for Unsaved

When I felt drawn by the sphere of darkness, and saw the very cloud of death part to receive me, I looked up to the paradisical heaven with a suppliant desire to enter there and be saved. But little did I know that even then, were I permitted to enter as a member into the spirit thereof, that I should suffer excess of agony from the effects of the love and harmony of heaven upon me, so that my condition would involve me in perplexity and misery equal to the deepest hell. In this manner my mind quickly surveyed the entire scene, while pleading for relief, and I was enabled to fully realize my condition, and felt assured that all was lost, and that I was doomed to woe.

At length an angel said, "Marietta, thou art not lost. True, thy deformity is exposed; and thou art suffering by reason of the awakening of thy spirit so as to discern the true state of a discordant soul, and by contrast with goodness thou art brought to a sense of want. In this, perhaps thou wilt be the better prepared to realize the goodness of God in the provisions made for redemption through the Lord Jesus, whom all the heavens adore.

"When thou wast previously admitted into the society of the sanctified, thy discordant condition was mostly holden from thy sight, and thou wast, as a guest, permitted to receive the influence as an outer sacredness which, like holy dew, fell upon thee and watered thy thirsty spirit. But so perfect is the breath of holiness here that it touched thy inner life, all thy latent unfitness appeared in contrast; hence thy suffering. *In this also thou art in a measure enabled to discover the wisdom of a benevolent Creator in the bestowment of that Providence which causes spirits of like nature and tendencies, whose habits are established, to incline to like conditions and abodes, so that opposite elements of absolute good and evil, being separate, shall not enhance the misery or annoy the bliss of any class. And thus is revealed why no unclean thing can enter the Holy City, John, the Revelator, saw.* For into this sacred Temple, no unholy disembodied spirit could enter. Nor can any law of existence receive the gross, unsanctified soul within that city of interior life whence originated the soft and spirit stirring melody which so much affected thee, nor could the inhabitants of this blessed abode dwell with spirits unreconciled to God in the spheres of darkness. Marietta, behold the goodness of God in the law of being. *How palpable would appear the injustice of a Righteous Creator, should he doom to the pales of night, or permit any law to operate so that one of these little ones should perish by being attracted into the deadly magnetism of the abode of guilt, the regions of woe. Their tender and pure natures would writhe beneath the touch of the inflamed passions of those who are abandoned to the madness of insatiable desires. In very deed might God be considered unjust should his law thus expose the innocent. Likewise, there would be a manifest want of mercy in their disposition, should any unsanctified and discordant spirit be impelled, while in that state, into the element of harmony and holiness, since their sufferings must increase in proportion to the degree of light and Supreme Good that pervades the abode of the pure.*

A Gulf Between Good and Evil

"Herein is displayed the wisdom and goodness of God. No absolutely discordant element in the world of spirits

mingles with the pure and harmonious. And thus is fulfilled the Sacred Text which saith, when speaking of these conditions; 'He that is filthy let him be filthy still: he that is righteous let him be righteous still: he that is holy let him be holy still:' *that is, let there be a separation between the qualities of good and evil with the disembodied, and hence let those who are holy enjoy that without warring of evil elements, and let the unholy blend by the law of their affinities.* For in the nature of their existence, in contrast with that of the unrighteous, it is justly written that there is an impassable gulf fixed, since these extremes can in no wise blend. Hence it is again written, 'Whoso is born of God is born of love, and love has no likeness to hatred. Whoso is under the dominion of evil doth not love God.' If mortals did but realize this law they would strive against evil and cultivate righteousness in themselves, and thus through grace, be prepared for the spiritual lesson thou canst not now fully learn nor comprehend. What thou hast witnessed and what angels have taught thee, consider, when these scenes are past, *and make thou a wise improvement thereof, lest a greater evil, than to realize an entire unfitness for an everlasting inheritance with the Sanctified, befall thee.*

"And when thou art restored to external sense and action, look unto Jesus, who alone can prepare thee to return and enjoy the rapture, and engage with the worshipers in this abode of the blessed. Here thou hast learned that the unregenerate cannot become the companions of these spirits. Weep not, Marietta," said the angel, as I began to yield to grief, *"weep not, for a ransome is prepared; in a healing fountain thou mayest wash, by which all the impurity of thy being may be removed. In this rejoice greatly, since through great mercy, Redemption is offered, and those who could not otherwise attain to perfect joy, are exalted from prison vaults to mansions in our Father's Kingdom. For this grace the*

*saints in heaven praise God, nor cease day or night to
utter hymns of thanksgiving to Him who is their Redeemer.*"

Thus saying, the angel touched my forehead, and a
stream of light entered my being, and I arose. "Now,"
said the angel, "thou mayest listen to the soft notes of
the song sung by the infants, who are just admitted from
the temples of learning into this great centre dome of the
infant paradise of instruction."

Song of Infants Before Their Chief Guardian

With sweetness the music of the infant choralists
arose from their pure hearts, filling the expanse and
swelling into gentle waves, which harmoniously moved
along the atmosphere above. But grandeur was added to
the scene as I beheld them formed into bands, and uniting class with class, made one throughout—each class
being composed of equal numbers, each spirit glowing
with the holy fire of the sacred hymn.

Moving from band to band was a female spirit, clothed
in raiment pure and white. Upon her head was a crown
set with gems, which shone with the brightness of the
sun. In her left hand she held an open volume, in her
right, a sceptre. She appeared to observe every infant,
and to clearly distinguish every voice, so as to know the
relation of their different qualities to each other, and
thence to all. Likewise, her every movement was noticed
by the infants who sought to imitate her even as pupils
do their instructors in schools with men.

The parts of music performed were manifold, yet in
harmony; and the melody was the beauty of perfection.
As they sung, their spirit fingers moved over their soft
and mellow-toned harps, while all were increasingly inspired with confidence which, adding to the melody,
appeared to blend them into one great soul, whose breath
was the spirit and harmony of celestial love.

PART II. THE DRAMA OF REDEMPTION

CHAPTER XVI

THE FORLORN AND DOOMED BEING

Here another scene, varying in many parts, was presented to the infants who were congregated in the centre dome for that purpose, preparatory to their advance to the superior plain, where they were to commence a life of heavenly use, unfolding and never-ceasing attainments.

———

In order that you may better understand what I relate, and the object of the varied representations before the infants, it is necessary to add, that one mode of instruction in the spirit world is to reveal, by figures and scenes, the principles involved in the several lessons.

There is a law by which every principle, scene, tragedy, person, creature, color, or substance in any sphere necessary to be revealed, can be reflected as from a mirror in reflex galleries; from planetariums, upon which the likeness of every substance, form, or color in a system, is daguerreotyped; or they can be represented by panoramic and continuous, revolving views; and also by personages performing the several parts, and thus representing the various principles and actors in any scene.

By these means, spirits unlearned in scientific or artistic wisdom, in moral or spiritual laws, or the plan, structure, and movement of the intellectual, spiritual, moral, and physical universe, are enabled to receive the impression intended, so as to discern the character of all and every idea, substance, thing, organism, or entity conveyed. And so perfect are the representations, that while beholding them the mind conceives the reality, insomuch that whatever is reflected becomes a part of the understanding.

To fully state the principles involved, and to delineate the varied scenes and figures employed even in that primary school, is beyond my comprehension or capacity of narration; and it would require volumes to contain their statements were they written. I must therefore condense the relation to a summary view, and you must be contented with the brief account I give.

———

As the new scene opened, the light and glory that illumined the dome gradually withdrew, until a twilight like that which follows the setting sun in an autumnal evening, alone relieved and marked the outlines of the great city.

All was silence, and every being motionless, and nought relieved the stillness of the moment save the sweet whispering of a soft and gentle breeze, which, like some celestial zephyr, glided over and through the vast plain.

Drama of the Forlorn Being

After this great change in the appearance of all around, and a brief pause, there appeared in view a portion of earth resembling a moon-light landscape, in which was represented, as if in some back ground, and beneath overhanging clouds burdened with gloom, a subterraneous aperture where lay a human being wounded in many parts, and apparently expiring. Upon this object, who was struggling as if seeking relief from his suffering, every spirit fixed its ardent attention.

His efforts were fitful and convulsive, but in no wise adapted to his necessities, and his inability to extricate himself was clearly manifest from his demeanor. He strove to heal his wounds by administering what he

thought to be antidotes; but which, when tested, proved
inadequate, and, by contrary effects, enhanced his suffering, and if possible, added to his peril. He used various
instruments by which he hoped to discern the pathway
leading from his gloomy abode, and to build a passage
across the abyss which encircled him. But all failed, and
he fell back in utter despair. Then he sought to be reconciled to his fate.

Companions Vainly Seek to Help Him

While he lay languishing and helpless, I saw a group,
composed of an elderly female, youths, and children,
gather around him. They appeared to grieve on his
account, and endeavored to afford him some relief. They
tried to bind up his wounds, to raise his drooping head,
and to revive vitality throughout; but all to no purpose.
He still groaned and languished. I now saw that he lay
more directly upon the brink of the abyss, and that he
drew nearer each moment, as if moved by an invisible
and irresistible power. Oh! the intensity of that moment.
The elderly female drew near, and clasping her arms
around his neck, sought to remove him from his fearful
condition. The youths united in the effort, but all in
vain. Still he drew nearer the abyss. I also saw that
his body manifested the increasing effects of the malady,
until every part was one diseased mass. Finally yielding
to the destroyer, he lay senseless; then to my surprise
arose therefrom a being like unto the former, and yet
I knew it was not the physical man, but his spirit.

A Diseased Spirit

The spirit, as it stood above the prostrate form, seemed
connected, and was still more deformed and dire. Spiritual and moral disease was inwrought throughout, and
controlled each part with unyielding power. I perceived
also that the body and spirit were not separated, that

they still depended upon each other; and that wherein the body had failed to give manifestation of grief, the spirit, as a separate entity, was capable of making full display, and irresistibly gave full expression of the suffering of the being. As the body had yielded to the power of disease and pain, so the spirit also finally languished under the malady which was working within and throughout. While thus suffering, the spirit looked up, as if to petition aid from above, but a cloud of thick darkness overshadowed it. Then it looked wildly around, evidently seeking some place of refuge or source of relief. This resulting as before, the spirit sank away, as if yielding in absolute despair, to the power of ceaseless wretchedness. As hope declined, the eye of the spirit vacantly fell, and in the downward look, discovered an abyss yawning beneath. Then it was again convulsed, and sought to escape, but in vain. The scene was horrible. The agonizing, fruitless efforts, and the manifestation of final despair, combined to present a scene of wretchedness beyond human description. Suddenly the spirit disappeared, and the man gave signs of returning life and sense; but he only recovered to know again, in the outer man, excessive misery, and to more fully feel his forlorn state.

No Hope in Arm of Flesh

The group, encouraged by the manifestation of returning life, renewed their efforts to restore him. This, too, was futile. They had no power to assuage his grief, or restore the lost health of body or spirit. While they thus struggled, a light descended, and lo! I saw that they were also in like condition of body and spirit, save that the effect had not manifested itself in them so perfectly. Nevertheless, the result was equally as certain. This they began to perceive, whereupon they exclaimed, "Is there no help?" "No help in the arm of flesh," answered a voice familiar to me, but I knew not whence it came. "Can the Ethiopian change his skin or the leopard his spots?" continued that voice. "How shall the unstrung instrument tune itself?—Yea, how shall the dying, those who are already victims, restore departing vitality? Shall they escape the doom awaiting them by the strength of their prostrate energies? Nay, where'er they go, there is no relief. Help must descend from above, or hope shall not appear."

Man Cannot Save Himself

As the scene closed an angel addressed the multitude saying, "The gloomy region just revealed is a view of earth, the birth place of mortals. The forlorn being, that of man, who there suffers unnumbered ills, physical, moral and spiritual, and who often struggles to overcome and to arise above them.

"His ineffectual efforts reveal his inability to save himself.

"The spirit which arose as the body yielded, represents the immortal nature which though the body perish shall exist in a more acutely sensitive state, and its sinking in despair, portrays the great truth that the death of the body can in no wise relieve the soul from moral or spiritual degradation.

"The group of friends represent human sympathy, which inclines members of the race to seek relief from sorrow, by mutual aid; that principle which prompts the more benevolent and philanthropic to devise means and to prosecute plans for the alleviation of the sufferings of man.

"Those, who indulge this principle feel another's woe. They deeply sympathize with those who endure pain and anguish from whatever cause. But being in like condition, and by seeking to remove evil from the world, and to elevate man through human devices and in their own strength, fail in the result although apparent relief may inspire transient hope. From this cause the race has struggled without success in unnumbered reformatory measures. For this reason, earth's reformers have encountered repeated failures until disheartened they sink into despair; and are often finally led to discover fundamental want in themselves.

"Thus hath it been with man from age to age. Periods have succeeded periods, and each have had their philanthropists who have struggled through a weary existence, but without attaining the goal of their purpose.

Failure of Human Remedies

"Oft the race, to human appearance, has approached the dawn of a better day; and those who have labored to that end, have sung earth's jubilee. But ere they have emerged from the gloomy plains, they have felt the triumph of inbred disease. The ground upon which they stood, hath yielded to the pressure; and the muscle upon which they relied relaxed, quitting its hold. The rock became sliding sands, and the strength of their hope and effort, weakness. Thus, when they supposed victory won, the heights attained, sudden quaking has seized the world of mind, which in its convulsive throes, hath precipitated them into a still deeper abyss. Thus shall it ever be, until men cleave unto the Lord, who alone is a sure defence and a stronghold in the day of trouble— upon whose shoulders rests the government; and in whom, and by whom, all things subsist. The voice from above declared that help was not in the arm of flesh, was that of Truth, which ever seeks to reveal to man his true condition, and to awaken him to a sense of his degradation, and to enforce the doctrine of salvation through the Lord Jesus."

Angel's Prayer for Infants

Then raising his eyes toward the superior heavens,

the angel, in a meek, fervent and exalted manner, said:

"Father of All, let thy Spirit inspire these infant minds with understanding, that they may behold with profit the scenes which are to reveal the effects of sin in the world of discordance, whence they are; also the wonders of thy love in the means of salvation.

"Endow them with supporting grace while beholding the trials of their Redeemer, incident to his mission, and his passion while suffering the cruelty of those he seeks to save.

"Grant, O Lord our Redeemer, that these may be prepared to arise through degrees of life and understanding, to the heaven of youths, where thy glory is revealed in greater degrees of paradisical light, love, and ecstatic beatitudes.

"Let thy will be done by angels who delight to lead upward the little ones whom thou hast entrusted to their charge, so that thy glory may be reflected upon them in a manner well-pleasing in thy sight. Then shall their spiritual understanding be enlarged, and the love principles of their beings unfolded, and thy name, O thou Savior of Men—thou who art all and in all to us, the ministering servants of thy grace—be glorified in them evermore." "Evermore, amen," responded the guardian angels and instructors. "Evermore, evermore, amen," and the heavenly atmosphere reaccented it until the echo expired in the distance.

CHAPTER XVII

THE BABE OF BETHLEHEM

After a brief pause, a voice as from a distance said, "Be instructed by what is given. Truths connected with your race are revealed to your understanding. Receive the principles, seek to comprehend."

Then the choralists touching their golden lyres, chanted with loud voices, "Glory to God in the highest, and on earth peace and good will to men. Behold we bring good tiding of great joy which shall be unto all people, for upon earth is born in the city of David a Saviour, which is Christ the Lord."

Birth of the Saviour

Then was revealed, beneath a pale light, Bethlehem, the birth place of the Redeemer. The condition of the infants in Paradise, moving in the very glory of Divine Life, attended by angels expressly appointed, blessed by the Redeemer, sanctified with his love, and greeted with choral bands of the heavenly spheres, reflected a state greatly in contrast with that now being revealed, in which was represented the dreary world, and the circumstances attending that memorable event, the birth of Jesus of Nazareth.

The humble condition of Mary the mother of Jesus, while holding in her arms the infant, through whom Salvation alone could appear unto men, and in whom was revealed the untold goodness and love of God, reflected so clearly the truth, that not only the infants but all the angels, beholding the scene, manifested great emotion. After a short pause, the angel who before enforced the truths revealed, said, "Behold the birth place of the Redeemer, even Jesus whose glory illumines this temple. For you the Spirit of Redemption assumed this humble form of manifestation. Through his humiliation, who is the Savior, these favors are conferred, and heavenly mansions prepared for all who trust in his grace and are obedient to the law of Redemption. Adore him for he is worthy."

Justice and Mercy Meet in Christ

"We will adore him ever more," said the chief guardian; and the infants repeated, "We will adore him." And again all was silent. The scene more plainly revealed Mary, meekly resting upon the breast of Joseph, who pressed her to his heart, while she gently folded to her pure bosom the Babe of Bethlehem. Near them were a few Israelites in humble attitude, steadily looking upon the babe and its mother. Around them were an innumerable company of angels, but invisible to mortal vision. These held in their hands crowns, while their harps, which were untouched and silent, lay before them. Above them rested a cloud of glory, and out of that cloud proceeded a voice saying, "This is my beloved Son." And another voice said, "This day is made manifest the love of God to man, who is fallen, yea, who is dead in trespasses and in sin. Now salvation appeareth. Now truth moveth from the eternity of its existence, clothed in the garments of salvation. *Justice and Mercy meet upon the fallen orb, and over prostrate humanity embrace. Justice declareth against sin; thus the eternal Throne is vindicated, and the government of the Kingdom perpetuated; while Mercy pleadeth the cause of the sinner who is exposed to unremitting sorrow by reason of transgression.*"

"Let us bow down and adore the God of our Salvation," said the chief guardian, and all assumed an humble attitude; during which another voice from above spoke, saying, "It becometh thee to worship, yea, to bow down while infinite condescension is being revealed. Thus let all heaven adore." The humble attitude of the angels and the infant spirits added greatly to the solemnity of the occasion. Surely there was reverence — sincere acknowledgment of mercies bestowed. I was reflecting upon the true devotion manifested by the worshipers, when the chief guardian said, "We will arise. Behold a new scene draweth nigh;" and raising her eyes toward the higher heaven, she continued, "Be thou our help, O our Father, in whose life we exist; that we may understand what Heaven revealeth for our instruction; that we may know thy love and be prepared to do thy will ever more." "Amen," responded every infant, led by their separate guardians.

CHAPTER XVIII

JUSTICE AND MERCY

The former objects had passed away during the worship of the angels and the infants, and new ones appeared.

Justice Appears

A bright cloud rested but a little above the temple, and from that cloud descended a being who appeared omnipotent in strength. Justice, was written upon his majestic brow. His movement was like one supreme, at whose bidding worlds might flee away, and in whose hand universal law might pause, and her evolving energies slumber.

This august personage advanced toward a gloomy glen, encircled by huge mountains whose lofty peaks ascended far into the blue vault above. His demeanor indicated purpose.

As he drew very near what appeared the object of his pursuit, a dark cloud moved down the mountains attended by lightning in all the terror of wild display, as if the electric fountains were issuing from an ocean of igneous elements. Heavy thunderings shook the base of the massive hills. Fire, smoke, and tempest were emitted, while the elements seemed to madly embrace each other. The scene was frightfully terrific; but still Justice advanced, and the very lightnings seemed to wreath themselves into a diadem about his brow.

"Destruction" was now mirrored in superflaming letters, in the very lightnings, upon the clouds, and repeated by the stunning peals of thunder.

Beneath this awful display of angry elements, and the movement of Justice, the earth began to quake and give way.

At this moment, when the excitement had apparently reached its climax, from beneath the cloud, at the foot of the mountain, came a voice of lamentation, a voice of despair, saying, "Spare us; is there no hope?" "No hope," echoed the thunders, and Justice still advanced. "No hope," he repeated, as he raised his hand of might. "No hope, no hope," chimed the hoarse voice of contending elements. "We perish without hope," said the voice of wailing which grew still weaker and more suppressed. "Alas! alas! we perish unpitied," and in an instant was revealed the forlorn being and the afflicted group displayed in a former scene.

Over the prostrate man bent the trembling female as if to screen him from the tempest; but as she saw Justice raise his mighty hand, she fell back, exclaiming, "All is lost! No hope! We perish! Receive us, thou abyss!"

Dreadful was the suspense of that moment. Justice still advanced, as if to cut in pieces, to crush at once the forlorn man whose trembling hands were upraised in form of supplication,—by whose side, and around whom, were fallen his group of friends, alike helpless and suppliant.

At this period a voice from the burning cloud said:

Justice Must Execute Penalty of Violation of the Law

"Law's proceeding energies have been violated, and thence disturbed in thee, O man. And thinkest thou to trifle therewith, and not to suffer the consequences? Dost thou not understand that law, when opposed, worketh the destruction of the body in which it is violated? Moral law is the law of sense and goodness. Hast thou not violated? Yea, thou hast. Now ensue the dread effects, and thou art the sufferer."

Mercy Pleads the Cause of the Sinner

As this voice ceased, superior light flashed over the scene, and from above a cloud exceedingly bright descended, from which came, with the speed of thought, another being, the very image of meekness, whose demeanor was the very opposite of Justice; and embracing Justice, who was still advancing toward the fallen group, said:

"Art thou inexorable, O thou who vindicatest the everlasting throne? Must the sinner perish? Is there no hope?" "No hope in the arm of flesh," answered Justice in a voice that shook the firmament above. The very stars trembled, and the earth quaked and reeled as the words proceeded from his lips. "No hope or cause of hope exists upon the fallen orb," again repeated Justice, still advancing. And as the blow was about descending upon the sinner, the being who hung upon the neck of Justice bent over that bleeding form, and placing her left hand upon his heart, raised the right, and touching the arm of Justice, said, "Thy Throne, O God, endureth for ever. Thy kingdom is from everlasting to everlasting. Thy Word endures. To thy years there is no end. Thou, O God, art holy. Righteousness is the foundation of thy throne—the pavilion of thy dwelling-place—the glory of the everlasting hills—the defence and safety of the Heaven of heavens, where congregate the unnumbered myriads of glorified seraphim. Here, O God, is a fallen being. Sin is the violation of thy law. The sinner hath presumed upon thy government, and touched with impious hands the flaming sword; hath dared vengeance; trifled with thy will; and contended with eternal and irrevocable justice. He hath fallen. He lieth bruised, mangled and expiring. Yet, O God, thou hast created him an immortal being; intellectual, hence accountable; spiritual, hence by sin he lieth upon the verge of a bottomless abyss, where, if he fall, he shall feel immortal pangs, and dwell in unremitting woe. The reed is bruised, but not entirely broken; the flickering blaze of the smoking flax, though expiring, still exists. Mercy is my name.

Mercy is an attribute of thy throne. To thee, O God, belong Justice and Mercy! Let thy love, O Eternal, descend! and thou, Justice, spare, O spare this fallen being! Spare him though he hath sinned, and bartered for a morsel his eternal good!"

Here Mercy bowed her head, as if to wait the decision and a voice from the cloud said, "Mercy, thou hast plead for the sinner, and heaven giveth audience. Canst thou find a ransom? Justice, pause in thy execution."

Christ Pleaded as Reason for Mercy

Then another voice said, "God so loved the world that he gave his only begotten Son. He shall bear their iniquity. By my righteous servant I will justify many."

Then there was a pause, during which, from the right approached a female—even Mary whom I had seen with the beasts of the stall pressing to her bosom the babe of Bethlehem—and by the expiring form bowed, over which by the aid of Mercy she extended the babe, and with reverence looked up toward the cloud. And the voice continued, "This is my beloved Son, in whom I am well pleased. A bruised reed shall he not break, and smoking flax shall he not quench, until he send forth judgment unto victory. And in his Name shall the Gentiles trust."

Then replied Justice, "Hath he endured temptation, and suffered without the Gate? Hath he conquered death? Can he stay the tempest of warring elements? Can he change the malign nature of that perverted heart? Can he descend the maelstrom of death, and arrest the heavy tide whose broad current thence rolls to the bottomless abyss?"

Then said Mercy, "The future shall answer thee, O, thou who holdest the balances of equity, the scales of universal right."

When Mercy had answered, the scene changed, and upon the mount, called the Mount of Olives, I saw a being more lovely than the sons of men. He lifted up his eyes to heaven and said, "Lo! I come, in the volume of the book it is written of me, to do thy will, O God!"

Then appeared a vast multitude of deformed beings exhibiting every type of human suffering and shameful depravity; and addressing them He said: "If any man thirst, let him come unto me and drink. I am the Way, the Truth and the Life. No man cometh unto the Father but by me." Whereupon another voice said, "This is the Son of David, the hope of Israel, the bright and Morning Star. Now ariseth the Sun of Righteousness. Now appeareth Truth in its redeeming glory from the Eternal Cause. Look unto Him, ye who perish, for lo! He cometh to redeem."

The Shepherd Seeks the Lost Sheep

Again I saw the mangled form. These words had fallen upon his dull and heavy hearing, and although he scarcely understood them, he raised his eyes as if to see whence hope was proffered. And as he looked, He who stood upon the Mount descended and bowed over him saying, "What dost thou desire?" And the sufferer said, "Oh that I might find salvation!" Then answered the Personage bending over him, "I came to seek and save the lost." Then said Justice to Mercy, "Where is thy ransom?" And another voice said, "Behold the Lamb of God which taketh away the sin of the world." And he who proffered redemption said, "For this cause came I into the world." "Even so," said an angel, "by thy stripes is the sinner healed."

"But," replied Justice, "Hath he prevailed?" Then addressing Mercy he continued, "Know, thou who pleadest the sinner's cause, that until he whom thou proposeth as Redeemer shall approach the fallen, holding in his hand these contending elements, he shall not rescue. Seekest thou still the fallen being's salvation, his restoration to harmony?"

"Yea," answered Mercy, "for this I interpose."

CHAPTER XIX

THE BETRAYAL

Another scene appeared; and O how inefficient are all means of communication to reveal to human minds its true character! First I saw that same lovely Being seated, with a company of his friends, around a table, one of whom leaned upon his breast, and in pure love's tenderest expression looked up into his face while listening to the words that fell from his lips. Mournfully and filled with exceeding sorrow, the group looked upon him as he said, "Verily I say unto you, one of you shall betray me." After which he took bread and blessed it, and break it, and giving it to them said, "Take, eat; this is my body. For you my body shall be broken." He then took the cup and gave thanks, and gave it to them, saying, "Drink ye all of it; for this is my blood of the New Testament, which is shed for many for the remission of sins. But I say unto you, I will not drink henceforth of the fruit of the vine, until that day when I drink it new with you in my Father's Kingdom."

Then I heard a mighty angel whose voice was like the utterance of Nature when her forces contend saying, "The Son of Man goeth as it is written of him; but woe unto that man by whom the Son of Man is betrayed: it had been good for that man if he had not been born!"

"Woe to that man; for him it had been good not to have been born. Woe, woe, woe be unto that man!" broke forth in a heavy voice which from many millions in univocal speech, pronounced the woe, and the elements of the interior shook like the leaves of a forest when contending with autumnal tempests.

As the echoings of these awful utterances which rolled along the bosom of the deep interior ceased, the little band arose, and after they had sung a hymn of solemn movement, retired.

Judas the Betrayer

Then I saw one of the number, silently and unperceived, withdraw from the band, as they retired slowly and solemnly from the scene of the last supper, and as he advanced, his movement changed, his step was quick and excited, his visage manifested an inward commotion that burned with consuming fires, fires kindled in the soul by antagonistic elements. At this I wondered. Nor could I perceive by what means a transition so sudden and so great could be effected. Just before, I had seen him seated with his friends, and those friends were suffering greatly by reason of the predictions of him to whom they looked for counsel and for safety. They mourned, fearing his departure from them. They leaned upon him as a dependent child leans upon a faithful parent. They had hoped, yea, had exalted their hope in him. The extent or exact nature of that hope I could not comprehend. Still I saw that in him they had placed great dependence for future good or great achievements. And when his words, which indicated his departure, had been spoken, they had fallen into despair, and perfect wretchedness possessed them when he declared that one of them should betray him. I heard them in the deepest solicitude inquire, "Lord, is it I? Lord, is it I?" That had been an awful moment in which gloom gathered around them as a mantle of thick darkness.

The Grieving Disciples

In their spirits they grieved, when he said, "A little while and ye shall not see me; and again a little while, and ye shall see me, because I go to the Father. But because I have said these things unto you sorrow hath filled your heart. Nevertheless, I tell you the truth. It is ex-

pedient for you that I go away. For, if I go not away, the
Comforter will not come unto you; but if I depart I will
send him unto you. I will not leave you comfortless. I
will come unto you. Let not your heart be troubled: ye
believe in God, believe also in me. In my Father's house
are many mansions: if it were not so I would have told
you. I go to prepare a place for you. I will come again
and receive you unto myself; that where I am there ye
may be also. Yet a little while and the world seeth me no
more: but ye see me: because I live ye shall live also.
Verily, verily, I say unto you, that ye shall weep and
lament, but the world shall rejoice: and ye shall be sorrowful, but your sorrow shall be turned into joy. And
indeed ye now have sorrow: but I will see you again, and
your heart shall rejoice, and your joy no man taketh from
you. These things have I spoken to you in proverbs: but
the time cometh when I shall no more speak unto you in
proverbs, but I shall show you plainly of the Father."

These words of promise and of consolation, which he
spake while predicting his departure, they believed; still
they were sad and exceeding sorrowful, because he said,
"I go away."

They loved him: he was worthy of all holy affection.

His words were full of goodness; and there was so
much of heavenly love, tenderness, and paternal care
manifested by him, that my wonder was excited while
seeking for a reason sufficient to induce any one of that
little company to withdraw from it that he might betray
into the hands of enemies, a Being whose presence thus
inspired hope, love, reverence, and adoration.

While my spirit pondered, I heard the angels who
instructed the infants say, "In what thou seest behold the
nature of good and evil contrasted. That little band was
the company of the Lord's disciples who partook of the
passover with him, the evening before his betrayal. He
who addressed them was the Redeemer, who, knowing

that his 'hour' was at hand, and also who should betray him, prepared their minds for the trial, and predicted the events which were to follow. He who so strangely withdrew, was Judas Iscariot, who betrayed his master for thirty pieces of silver.

"Observe more minutely this scene as it passes, and the two great principles which are operative with man in a fallen state, shall so unfold themselves as to impress thee with its purpose, and ingraft thy being with the solemn truths unfolded."

The angel again withdrew, and he who was called Judas appeared, and was seen just entering a council-chamber, where were gathered the chief priests and elders of ancient Israel, who at the time of the Lord's passion, conspired to take him and put him to death, and thus bring upon him perpetual scorn and blasting ignominy. And, oh! how changed, how entirely changed! His spirit was the opposite of that which had appeared in the room set apart for the Last Supper. His outward expression bespoke inward rage,—the rage of a malicious heart, a heart grievously treacherous and desperately wicked. At this time a pale light flashed over his head, which revealed a group of demoniac spirits. These urged him onward by their vindictive inspiration. They manifested all that can be conceived as the embodiment of evil which composes the elementary being of the arch-fiend; the foe of all good; the destroyer of peace; the instigator of crime; the enemy of right; the soul-alluring Satan. These poured forth their fiendish, yea, their hellish magnetism, and by the power of their will surcharged him with the hate they desired to manifest toward the Son of Man.

Judas' Rendezvous With the Priests

As he entered the mimic sanctum, the priests arose, and with smiles, such smiles as malice, with a hope of revenge inspires, greeted him. Then the chief priests, addressing him, said, "Welcome, Judas, friend of right, friend of God's ancient Church, the law of Moses and the people of this ecclesiastical kingdom. He whom the rabble call Jesus, and who by his followers is called the King of the Jews, by his dictum, has long been worthy of death. He has sought the destruction of this beloved city, the city especially favored of God. And the great temple he has prophesied to destroy; to put down the authority of the Church; to change laws and customs; upon the ruin of Jehovah's kingdom to establish his own. He calleth himself God. He is a blasphemer against high Heaven, and mocks the throne of the Eternal. He presumes to call us hypocrites; even those whom God, by his right hand, hath exalted as teachers in Israel, he calleth blind leaders of the blind. He hath charged us with having the keys of the kingdom, and by our love for sin refusing to enter into life; and by a vile nature and love of power, of keeping those from entering who are willing. Surely he is worthy of death." "Yea, worthy of the most ignominious death," responded in unison all who were present.

"This man is drawing with him the credulous, the ignorant, the visionary, and those who are dissatisfied with the Church," continued the priest; "and by his peculiar nature adapted to work wonders, he hath deceived many who are worthy of a better calling." Then addressing his friends, he continued: "But these will soon become conscious of his false character and well shall it be for him who first discovers to us the true character and resort of this vile deceiver, and shall enable us to bring him before the people. Upon such a one the nation shall bestow great honors, and lasting blessings shall be upon his head." "And lasting blessings shall be upon his head," repeated the associate priests.

This was sufficient to inspire Judas with the desire of being first in the undertaking. Whereupon he proposed, in presence of them all, to deliver his Master into the hands of any band the priest should then commission for that purpose, upon the condition—which appeared to have been previously considered—of his receiving thirty pieces of silver.

Gethsemane

Again the scene changed. The mantle of evening overshadowed that portion of Earth. A little way from the busy multitude I saw him who had counselled his disciples, moving slowly along with three of his chosen. He was sorrowful. I can never forget that scene. Oh! the loveliness that was manifest. Truly I thought him the chiefest among ten thousand, and the one altogeher lovely. Still he suffered. They paused, and he said, "My soul is exceeding sorrowful even unto death: tarry ye here and watch with me. Pray that ye enter not into temptation." He then left them and went a little farther, and fell upon the ground. And while bowing upon the cold earth, enduring the deepest agony, he prayed more earnestly; and his sweat was as it were great drops of blood falling down to the ground.

Above him the heavens opened, and legions of angels appeared, apparently clothed in habiliments of mourning. They veiled their faces as they bent over the garden of Gethsemane, in which their Lord suffered. All was silent, mournfully silent. There was Christ the Lord, the Divine Man, he whose name is written in the Scriptures as the Wonderful, Counsellor, the Mighty God, the Everlasting Father, the Prince of Peace.

While observing the Savior in his agony, a cloud descended, resting over the Redeemer, in which were Justice and Mercy. They observed with intense interest the scene below.

At length the Savior prayed, saying: "O my Father, if it be possible, let this cup pass from me. Nevertheless not as I will, but as thou wilt." Then said Mercy to Justice, "Here is the Ransom."

Again he prayed, "O my Father, if this cup may not pass away from me, except I drink it, thy will be done." Then there descended a mighty angel, who stood by him, and strengthened him.

Then Mercy said to Justice, "Behold the offering."

The Betrayal

The hour of suffering having passed, Jesus arose, and going to his disciples and finding them asleep, said unto them, "Sleep on now, and take your rest; behold the hour is at hand, and the Son of Man is betrayed into the hands of sinners."

"Behold, in Jesus," said my guide, addressing herself to me, "an example of meek submission. From his sympathy with the deranged and dying race, he agonized beneath the burden of human woe. Though just, he suffers, by reason of an adopted affinity with the unjust; and still thou didst hear him say, 'Not as I will, but as thou wilt; not my will, but thine, O God, be done.'

"This is needful that man may have grace vouchsafed, and by the power of love become united to heavenly spheres, and thus be exalted from degradation to mansions of righteousness and peace, prepared in heaven for the ransomed of the Lord. But, Marietta, thou shalt soon behold the contrast; in what is to pass before thee shall be unfolded the true condition of the perverted heart."

Again my attention was directed to a dark and doleful scene. Below me I beheld a heavy cloud, which was agitated as if burdened with the spirit of wrangling elements. Discordant sounds arose from the midst thereof. They were hard to be understood, and at first the cause was hidden from me. But at length I heard, as from the voice of an excited rabble, the enthusiastic inquiry, "Where shall we find him? Hasten, most worthy guide, to the place of his retreat. Time wasteth, and the leaders of the people demand the 'outlaw.' He shall perish." "Yea, he shall perish, and that speedily," clamored a multitude who were, while moving toward Jesus and his disciples, enveloped in a cloud that overhung their pathway. The contrast between the scenes was so great, that I was terrified, and turning to my guide I inquired, "Who are these that disturb the stillness of this solemn hour? And canst thou inform me whence they are, and whither bound? Of whom do they speak in language so excited, and with a determination so destructive?"

"These," she said, "are a band of soldiers from the chief priests and elders of the Jews. The object of their revengeful pursuit is Jesus, who, in the agony of his soul, prayed in the garden."

"What hath he done to excite such envy," I exclaimed.

"He hath preached the year of the Lord, and announced the mission of God's only Son to the world. He hath given sight to the blind, restored the deaf to hearing, healed the sick, raised the dead, comforted the mourner, instructed the ignorant, and pleaded with the despisers of the mercy of God to regard the Creator of heaven and earth as their Sovereign, Rightful Lawgiver, Heavenly Father, and Redeemer."

"And is this that for which they seek to destroy him?" I inquired. "Hath he never contended with them?"

"Hast thou not read in the Sacred Text that which the prophet spake, when moved by the Holy Ghost, concerning One that should come, 'Behold my servant whom I have chosen, my beloved in whom I am well pleased. I will put my spirit upon him and he shall show judgment unto the Gentiles. He shall not strive nor cry; neither shall any man hear his voice in the streets.' This Jesus, who in his humility, bowed in prayer, and whom the populace seek to destroy as a vile outlaw—God manifest in the flesh—is He of whom the prophet spake.

While the angel yet spake, the exasperated throng, armed with swords and staves, approached Jesus and his disciples; and lo! they were led by one of the company who sat with him at the last supper, even Judas Iscariot, the same who had left his Lord and proposed to deliver up Jesus to the chief priests and elders of the people. As they drew near, I saw above Judas a mighty angel of darkness, from whom issued a pale sulphuric flame that encompassed him and burned in his nerves like living fire. With wild determination Judas advanced and hailed Jesus as his friend and Lord, sealing his mockery and heartless treachery with a kiss. But Jesus appeared fully to comprehend his design, and addressing him said, "Friend, wherefore art thou come?" And to the multitude he said, "Are ye come out as against a thief, with swords and staves, to take me? I sat daily with you, teaching in the temple, and ye laid no hold upon me. But if ye seek me, let these who believe in me go their way. For this cause I came into the world." Then answered one of the multitude, "Tell us for what cause." "That salvation might be given to the world, and that all, even those who assail me, might, through faith and repentance, enter into rest. Into your hands I submit myself, but these my disciples, no harm shall befall them." Then said the mockers, "Thou art our prisoner, and we bear thee before the tribunals of the people, and no one helpeth thee; how sayest thou then of these thy disciples, 'No harm shall befall them?' "

At this the disciples fled, every one his own way, and forsook him, save one who followed his Lord even unto the judgment hall.

CHAPTER XX

CRUELTIES INFLICTED UPON JESUS

Then with cruel hands they led him away amid the shouts of the rabble.

As this scene was closing, I turned and looked upon the infants and angelic spectators, who appeared more afflicted than at any former period. I then inquired, "Can there be sorrow in heaven? Do angels weep?" When I heard a voice say, "Well, Marietta, dost thou inquire. Angels have hearts to feel. And who in heaven could witness the manifestation of the betrayal of the Savior of sinners without a soul poured out in sad expressions?" "Amen!" uttered ten thousand voices. "And who can endure the sight? Behold the innocent sufferer. See! see! they beat him as they hurry along the rugged way. They mock, they deride him; they cruelly treat him. Let all the heavens pause as they behold the mournful scene; for lo! the Redeemer suffers in the hands of sinners. Awake, ye spirit sympathies; lo! Divine Good whom angels adore is despised and rejected of men."

As the voice ceased, I heard another angel say,—"Lo! from the highest heavens angels descend."—And I beheld far above the vast assemblage that witnessed the scene, an innumerable company of superior beings. They had palms in their hands and crowns upon their heads; and their crowns represented the starry heavens, being a miniature expression of the wreathed universes which encircle the throne of the Infinite. As they drew near, a dazzling light preceded them which pervaded the spiritual atmosphere, and was so exalted in its nature that the angels of the highest order who had composed the former audience could not steadfastly behold it. The approach of this light so revealed the imperfection of my nature that I sought to conceal myself; but nothing could be concealed in that holy light. I fain would have fled, but I had no power to control that desire. Surely, I said in my mind, if this is but a manifestation of what is in the higher heavens, how can mortals ever attain to that divine abode? *How can vile man hope to enter that glory, which to the unprepared soul, would surely become a consuming fire?*

While thus reflecting, I heard one of the cherubic beings say, "Angels, kindred spirits, inhabitants of the exalted heavens! bow down before your Lord, for He is worthy. Adore Him from the deep and immortal sentiment of your revering spirits; for lo! all angels delight to offer praises unto Him. He is worthy of all adoration. Praise Him! Praise the Lord, the Redeemer of Earth! While fallen beings mocking gather around Him and impiously hail Him King, let the harmonious universe be moved with reverence, and all intelligences humbly adore."

Then each bowed down in silent adoration, while feeble and bewildered men hasten him to the judgment hall. As the angels declared him God manifest in flesh, I wondered still the more that having power, he did not exert it and subdue those who sought to destroy; and also, as there were myriads of mighty angels, each having apparent capacity to disperse at will those who led their Lord away, that they too did not seek to avert the impending storm. Perceiving my thoughts the instructor said, "He came to seek and save, and not to destroy; he endureth the scoffs of the wicked, and offereth himself a ransom for sinners; and by his submission fulfilleth that prophecy which saith, A bruised reed He shall not break —He will not harm the helpless—and smoking flax He shall not quench—He will not extinguish the life or hope of man.—His is a mission of redemption, and not of judgment and execution."

Then I heard voices as the going forth of many waters, saying, "Be amazed, O Earth! for thy sins have brought upon thee unutterable woe, and pity hath prompted the offering, and thy Redeemer groaneth beneath the load."

The Ransom

Then said Mercy to Justice, "God as has been written, so loved the world that he gave his only begotten Son, a Ransom. This is the Ransom. In Jesus the nations of earth shall have hope. Behold the offering. In this offering there is a principle for the removal of sin and unholiness; and to establish a sympathy between the depraved race and that life which is above.

Then said the angel to the infants, "This is your Redeemer. *In him alone is that Life which can quicken and save, and by him you were admitted into this paradise. Let each observe the scene as it shall advance, for by it Heaven purposeth to give an impression which shall enable all to estimate, according to their capacity, the value of the Redeemer to them.*" While the angel addressed them, their expression of sympathy displayed the purity of their being, and the tenderness and emotion with which they had observed the suffering Son. Then all with one accord said, "How shall we utter praises and thanksgivings to God, for this gift, the gift of life through his only begotten Son, our Savior?"

"Could we not relieve him? Can we not share his woe? Lo! he is in the midst of his foes. They know him not. They give him needless pain. Who can endure the sight? Let us fly to his relief!" exclaimed the multitude. "He is our Redeemer!" fell from the holy lips of the occupants of the infant paradise.

"He is our Lord; He maketh the heavens harmonious with the perfection of his being, and melodious with the euphony of his speech. He maketh bliss to arise as the golden morning, and shed its holy lustre and Divine Good upon the workmanship of his hands. Lo! the heavens declare his adorable name, and the peopled expanse vibrates with the soft and gentle cadence of his proceeding love. Yet in form of Divine Man we behold him hurried onward by fallen beings, as they bear him through discordant elements toward the haughty sanhedrin of a heartless church—a church where Jehovah is named in empty sound, but not worshiped." Thus spake one of the mighty angels in the audience of the multitude which man could not number. Then as the voice of one man they uttered, "Let us arise and beat back the mockers of the Lord."

"Nay," said another voice; and I looked, and behold Justice stood in a cloud of exceeding brightness, holding the seven thunders in his right hand, from which issued lightnings and tempest, and these overspanned the globe, and enveloped the race both small and great, the living and the dead, in its awful cloud, and shook the foundation of earth, and caused the souls of men to quake with the greatness of the terror of the rolling thunderings and blackening tempests. And in his left hand he held a scroll, whereon was written in separate sections, an abridged expression of the eternal law of spiritual, moral, and intellectual being—abridged according to, and complying with the capacity of man, and in all respects adapted to his condition and necessity. Before him was the deformed being before revealed, wounded nigh unto death, and the blood from his wounds stained the earth whereon he lay.

Again repeated Justice, "Not so, the soul that sinneth must die. The result of violated law is irrevocable." Then I saw Mercy advance, and enter the tempest, and bending over the wounded being, in manner as on a former occasion, said, "Lo! He who was, and is, and is to come, descendeth to Earth, and by the incarnation of the Spirit, shall renew that sympathy with men which shall exalt them from their fallen condition, and restore the ruined soul, and harmonize by the perfection of his being the discordant race with eternal law; and then in him shall be perfected that reunion which shall restore the lost planet. And here," Mercy again repeated, "Behold the ransom."

Justice Demands Christ to Tread Winepress Alone

"Even so," said Justice, "the Offering is presented. But it is in the law of existence, and accepted in the law of grace, that he shall tread the winepress alone.— And these," addressing himself to the angelic hosts, "seek to rescue the Offering, and prevent the issue."

Then said Mercy to the astonished millions, "Thus it behooves Christ to suffer. Keep ye the awful suspense, as ye witness the effects of sin upon the sinner's sense and consciousness of right. Lo! the conflict heightens, and the Son of Man shall engage in warfare with the powers of death." Then said the multitude, "Permit that we do not witness the scene. Who can endure it?"

"Nay," said Justice, "should not the heavens behold and wonder, and Hades quail beneath the awful tread, as the God-Man proceeds to enter the death-gate, and conquer the foe of man, and bring life and immortality to light." "Amen," answered all who beheld and heard, "Even so let thy will, thou Eternal Spirit, in heaven and earth, and by us and all intelligences, be done, now and evermore; ever, evermore. Amen."

"Even so, let all heaven respond," said Justice, "that God shall be all and over all, now, henceforth, and for ever." "Amen! hallelujah! hallelujah! amen!" answered the meek observers of the scene: "Evermore thy will be done! Amen!"

CHAPTER XXI

CHRIST BEFORE TRIBUNAL

As the voices ceased, the conspiracy against the Lamb of God arose as from a smoking pit, and appeared above the throng of mortals, in the form of a demon of gigantic dimensions. Upon his head were many horns, each of which emitted a volume of lurid flame, which, like a cloud, enveloped that portion of the earth in the burning magnetism of fiendish hate. Upon his forehead was written, "Crucify him, crucify him; for he is not worthy to live. He is a seducer of the people." And upon his breast was written, "Apollyon;" or the "Manifestation of Enmity to Good." Upon his heart was seen in blazing characters, "Jesus shall not triumph; but death shall doom him to the tomb where mortals slumber, and inactivity reigns. There he who has called himself the Son of God, and made himself equal with God, shall feel the death-fetters of my irrevocable decree. Then I will dash his followers upon the rocks of human prejudice; gloom, and oppression, and dismay shall be their lot throughout all ages."

"Hear ye this," said a sepulchral voice, "hear ye this," hissed ten thousand serpent-tongued demoniac visages, while the vault below quivered as if some mighty potentate of a nether region had, with his blazing sceptre, touched the fountain, the mighty deep.

Death and Hell Combine

Then arose out of the pit a flame, which, although concealed from mortals, ascended amid this throng, causing the sphere of their being to blend and burn like mingling flames; and as each appeared a self-supporter of the fiery element, so by coalescence the intensity was increased until the host presented the appearance of a burning destructive tempest. This, as a magnetic principle, pervaded the congregation of mortals, who were instruments in the external, inspired to consummate the merciless and fiendish design upon Jesus, the meek and humble sufferer.

"The battle heightens," said an angel, who stood above the tempest in the atmosphere of heavenly purity; "With wonder, all ye heavens, behold the scene. Now death and hell combine; now the powers of evil charge upon the God-Man, who, while contending with the united force of enmity and destruction, by reason of sympathy with the race of mortals, is weighed down with the sorrows and sins of men."

"And," said another voice, "who shall determine the issue? for, lo! myriads of the servants of evil congregate, and mortals who surround the sufferer are becoming like those who inspire them.

Before the Tribunal

Then I saw them lead Jesus into the audience-chamber of the rulers of the people. Upon his head was a platted crown of thorns. His temples were pierced, and blood ran down his cheeks. His hands were also bound. He did not murmur, but looking upward moved his lips as if speaking. Suddenly the host that had arisen from the pit, fell back as though smitten by some mighty hand, and exclaims, "Lo! he speaks with God! and with pity beholds the multitude of mockers. The issue is not equal. Our prompter is hate, malice, revenge; his is love, meekness and submission. Flee we must from the power of that gentle Spirit. It is the deepest hell to endure his tenderness, and we cannot contend with his love."

Then again appeared the special manifestation of Evil in gigantic form; and he stretched forth his hand, from which proceeded a dark volume of self-consuming elements, and in a voice of terror said, "Arise! enter the combat, for now is the battle set! What, though he looks upon his tormentors in love, I have turned many hearts of love into hate; many calm spirits into madness; many a praying soul into the utterance of blasphemy. He shall not prevail, for now the conflict approaches the consummation period. This day, by my own hand, I will achieve for myself immortal victory." Thus saying, he prompted a mortal, who approaching Jesus as he stood among his accusers, smote him with the palm of his hand.

Then I heard a movement as if the heavens above had fallen. I looked, and lo! all the angels were upon their knees, and bowing their heads, raised their snow-white and spotless hands toward heaven; heaven was in mourning.

Then again I saw one approach Jesus saying, "Art thou the Christ? art thou the King of the Jews?" And Jesus answered, "Thou sayest it." And lo! the power of darkness gave way, for his voice disturbed the regions of death, and all was silent.

Justice Explains

"He, your Redeemer," said an angel to the infants in grief, "is smitten by the impious agent of the sphere of death, and his temples pierced by the crown of thorns. By this, evil is represented. It is its element, its determination, to smite the manifestation of good, and without that disposition it could not exist. These vile beings that arise from their nether abode, and like a cloud from some smoking pit darken the earth, are those evil spirits, that torment the sons of men. Filled with lust, and unable to indulge the propensity, they seek to vent their insatiate passions in vengeance upon bewildered mortals. And as Jesus shall rescue the humble soul from their power, and as he is the manifestation of the Incarnate Spirit, and his mission with men, in the condition of a Redeemer is to sever the power of the enchanter and break in pieces his kingdom which is established with men, so the prince of the power of darkness shall seek to conquer him, and dash in pieces, like a broken potsherd, the Kingdom of Peace which he shall establish on earth.

"Moreover, here the two principles meet. Death and hell arise, from the nether magazine; raging with the inextinguishable fires of pride and fiendish hate, and being convinced that the decisive hour is at hand, prompted by that embodiment, called Satan or Deceiver, they venture the engagement. The theatre of action is the external world, for there the condition of men renders them susceptible to influences from the spheres of good and evil.

"Yea, more, they are intellectual beings, and responsible, hence moral beings condemned in transgression. Therefore the righteousness of God's Throne declares against the sinner; so then Justice,—and Justice is my name,—must also be maintained if the violator live. Man must perish, or through some wise provision there must be a medium or mediator between him and the law violated. To this end a Ransom has been proferred, as embodying all that is necessary to enter the great vortex of human degradation, and grasp the awful current, and stand amid the conflicting elements, while rescuing the sinner. And this can only be effected by the reversion of the movement of the destructive tendency of the race. Those arising from the pit unite this deadly tendency with the powers of death and hell; and therefore, to save the sinner, death and hell shall be held subject to the will of the Conqueror. The principle of evil shall be bound by Omnipotent and eternal Will. For the depraved race Mercy hath appeared, and in her arms bringeth a Ransom, saying on him God hath laid help, and that he is mighty and able to save. And lo! the Offering now descendeth the vortex."

Mercy Presents the Ransom

Then said a voice, "I am Mercy. I offer the Ransom." Again said Justice, "If he be able, he shall triumph over death, hell and the grave; but he shall not strive nor cry, neither in contention shall his voice be heard." Then, answered Mercy, "He is like a lamb for the slaughter, like a sheep dumb before her shearers, he openeth not his mouth." "Even so," said Justice, "and he shall also make his soul and offering for sin before he shall see his seed." Again, answered Mercy, "Although he descends the vortex of death, his days shall be prolonged, and the pleasure of the Lord, the work of Redemption, shall prosper in his hands." His Kingdom shall be an everlasting Kingdom, and to his Government there shall be no end; for through the Mediator, God shall be just in the salvation and justification of him that believeth." "Amen!" answered Justice. "Hallelujah, hallelujah, amen!" arose from spirits, angels and seraphs.

Then I heard Jesus say to him who inquired the nature and object of his mission, and who had referred him to the danger of his position, "For this cause came I into the world, that the world might be saved; and since no man can come to the Father but by me, I submit to the consequence of my mission." Then with great emotion Mercy lifted her eyes to the heaven above, and said, "Great is thy goodness, O God, since for the Salvation of the sinner the just entered death's dominion and rescueth the unjust." Then approaching Justice, she extended her hand saying, "Dost thou accept the Offering I bring as adequate?" Then Justice bowed over the bleeding form of humanity, which again appeared, and received the extended hand of Mercy, saying, *"When this Offering shall have in meekness endured unto the end, then the sinner shall be restored through repentance toward God and faith in the Lord Jesus."*

Chapter XXII

THE DREAM OF PILATE'S WIFE

Then I saw a company of angels descending from a celestial band, far above the scene, and, as if upon some errand of mercy where momentous consequences were pending, they proceeded to a palace in the city and paused above it, and one of them entered a room wherein was a lovely female, whose mind appeared anxious and disturbed, while she was meditating upon the scene which moved the exasperated populace. The angel did not appear to her external vision, but presently began to soothe her nervous form into quietude, and to induce a soft and gentle slumber. How soon, thought I, that weary agitated form has found quiet and repose, beneath the influence of an angelic being; and how free from exciting and disturbing care are the inhabitants of the blissful skies! She rested, and an angel breathed upon her the breath of pure angelic love.

Paradise

She awoke in the spirit and dreamed (as mortals term it) that she stood by a gentle river, garlanded with the floral beauties of a celestial paradise. The waters of the river were bright and transparent, upon the bosom of which was mirrored transcending beauty of the paradisical landscapes that skirted that living stream, and environed its pathway. The waters echoed the soft notes of the feathered choirs that rested in the branches of the immortal trees and floated in the spiritual ether above the floral plains.

Charmed to ecstatic delight, she lifted her hands as if in adoration, and as she raised her eyes she beheld innumerable companies of the inhabitants of the blissful abode, who had just paused in a song of angelic love, the echoing melody of which, reverberating in the holy skies, in their retiring anthems awoke the hearing of the enraptured dreamer. As she stood beholding the angels above her, she became conscious of the cessation of the harmonious utterance of the immortal inhabitants, and the melody of the myriads of paradisiacal birds, which died upon the ear. A death-like stillness held the whole realm as in the embrace of an awful suspense.

While seeking the cause the scene changed, gloom veiled the beautiful river; the floral inhabitants folded their expanded leaves, and dropped their aroma as tears that fell from the bowed and humbled stamens and folded cups. The forests stood still, not a leaf moved, for even the celestial breezes paused. The angelic hosts above had veiled their faces and a pale light, as if the image of sadness, occupied the place of the bright glory that had illumined the world around her. Her heart grew faint, her hands fell lifelessly by her side, her head dropped upon her breast, and with her face pale and the image of perfected sadness, she looked downward. Her eyes gave up their brilliancy and life seemed departing, when an angel touched her, saying, "Pilgrim, wherefore dost thou wonder? Art thou not of the city of Jerusalem, in the land of shadows and of night?"

The Warning

The dreamer, startled by the voice of the strange speaker, raised her head, and beheld before her one of the immortal inhabitants clad in mourning. Surprised, she sought at first to escape, when the angel continued, saying, "Fear not; for in this land no harm shall befall thee." I come a messenger from that innumerable company of angels thou didst behold above thee. My errand is one of mercy. Thou hast witnessed the glory, harmony, and melody of this divine abode. Such is the true state of the pure and ever blessed. These rivers, fountains, streams, blossoms, and all animate existence, unite in one expression of ceaseless praise. But thou hast witnessed the change; how vast and how sudden. Thou too, art sad, and would know the cause. For this I come to thee. We suffer with our Lord, who in thy city is this day arraigned before a depraved, vindictive, and mock tribunal. Our Lord, who there suffers, is the manifestation of the Divine Spirit, the Incarnation thereof, God manifest in flesh, in the person of Jesus. Him the Jews seek to crucify. He goeth, as it is written of him, but woe unto those his false accusers, vile blasphemers, and unjust prosecutors. And thou, spirit of the lost world, thou art interested; for, lo! thy husband, though conscious of the innocence of Jesus for the people, bartereth innocent blood. Go thou quickly to thy lord, fall before him, and warn him of his danger. Tell him what thou seest,—how the land where immortality reigns, mourns; yea, that every tree, plant, and flower thereof bows in sorrowful attitude, that the birds of Paradise fold their wings and wait in awful suspense, that the rivers, the transparent waters, wear a heavy gloom that veils their glory, that angels lay down their crowns, and drop their lyres, and are dumb, and fall down in sadness; while Jesus thy Redeemer stands before the heartless tribunal of fiendish men. Go, nor tarry, else a moment lost may doom Pilate, whom thou shalt seek to save." "Awake!" said the angel who had soothed her to silent slumber; and, lo! she arose quickly, startled, yea, terrified with her vision, and hastened to send to Pilate her husband, saying, "Have thou nothing to do with that just man; for I have suffered many things this day in a dream because of Him." But Pilate, disregarding her entreaties, yielded to the insane demands of the people, and condemned Jesus to the Cross, and gave him up to be scourged, then crucified.

CHAPTER XXIII

JESUS LED OUT TO BE CRUCIFIED

As the sentence was passed, and Jesus was being led out to be scourged, the veil that had for a brief period concealed the inhabitants of the regions of death from our view, was removed, and again the arch-demon and his hosts appeared. Then he raised his hand, from which issued a broad sheet of sulphuric flame that moved and flashed like unto a banner over the vaults below. Upon it was written, "Victory to Apollyon. This day have I prevailed with men, and they have condemned the innocent." Then I heard ten thousand hoarse sepulchral voices saying, "Hail, thou Prince of Darkness, all hail! Thou hast prevailed, and man shall feel the sting of death. Go up to victory! Go ye up; for lo! we arise from our nether abode, and witness the God-man as he shall writhe beneath the scorpion lash and agonize upon the Roman Cross." "Ah-ha, ah-ha!" arose in swelling volumes from the demoniac abodes below, and the air was rent with the loud acclaim uniting with the infernal chant from the mad populace that rushed to the scene of cruelty.

"And is it not enough?" cried a voice in manifestation of deep lamentation, "O Justice! art thou inexorable? is not the ransom made perfect? Must we endure the scene? Shall the innocent suffer at the hands of sinners longer? Spare, O spare! Lo! his back is torn with lashes! His temples bleed! His form trembles beneath the heavy burden! He groans in Spirit! Must the power of evil prevail?

Then Justice answered, "He entereth into suffering with the fallen race, and endureth until the time appointed. His life is not taken, but he giveth it for many;

and although Satan triumphed for a season, the strong man armed shall enter his abode."

The suspense continued until every being was absorbed and pervaded by its influence. Again Jesus stood before us; His form was disfigured, and he was weak and faint. Still they placed upon his mangled back the huge engine upon which to execute him, and forced him along, amid the shouts and jeers and blasphemies of the people, toward the place of crucifixion.

Until this time I had been dumb, made so by the awfulness of the varied and mingled scenes that were rapidly passing before me. But as Jesus trembled and reeled beneath his load, and while his body was bleeding from the cruel scourgings, and his temples were gored and swollen from the effects of the crown of thorns, and the maddening cry, "Away with him, crucify him, crucify him!" rolled over the city, I could endure no longer, and exclaimed to my guide, "Why will not Justice spare the innocent and let the guilty suffer? Let the world abide the consequence of violated law, nor let innocence endure the pain and woe necessary to that union with the sinner necessary to his salvation. O why shall this scene continue? Why shall Jesus bear the cross? Why shall the infatuated race be permitted to inflict pain upon the pure, yea, him who seeketh their good?"

Still Jesus moved slowly along, ready to fall, faint, weary and in agony. He spake no word, but looked with love and pity upon his tormentors. While I was reasoning and wondering, I discovered that he moved more unsteadily, less firm even than before, until he sank down beneath his burden. His humanity had failed, and as he yielded from his Spirit within him, he groaned, and all was still. For the first time, his persecutors and crucifiers paused in their cruelty, and manifested care for him; and I thought perhaps that apparent care was on account of fear that they should not enjoy his protracted suffering upon the cross, beneath which he now lay bleeding. As he faintly yielded, the effect upon the saints and angels was beyond any power to describe. Truly it appeared that the very heavens would fail, and happiness so far depart as never to be restored.

Justice Explains Result of Sin Uncontrolled

The scene had been increasing in its awful interest; but when Jesus yielded beneath the heavy load and the continued scourging, all the spirits moved as if they fain would have relieved him; whereupon a voice uttered from afar, "It is written of him, he treadeth the wine-press alone." "Even so," said Justice, "and let the inhabitants of earth, and the angels of heaven, know that he endureth for sinners. By his stripes they are healed. He entereth the death-gate, that thereby he may rescue those who, by transgression, have fallen." "Amen," answered Mercy, who now appeared above the Cross, "amen; he offered himself for sinners. Justice, here is the Offering I bring." "Thou hast said," replied Justice, "he suffers, but he suffers in the hands of those whom he seeks to rescue from the consequences of a law they have violated. It is no vindictive wrath inflicted from the Father of life, but the consequences of his mission, and the heart he seeketh to save, made malicious by inversion and evil inspiration. Let not the heavens above, or the earth beneath, or the lost who dwell beneath the earth, declare against the goodness of the Lord Creator; for it is the nature of sin thus to oppose and inflict, and seek to destroy good, or its manifestation, and in this sin is only made to appear in its unrestrained nature. Sin, uncontrolled, would blot out the universal sun, make the heavens a pandemonium of evil and malicious beings, break in pieces the government of the universal Lord Creator, and render void the moral principles and nature of universal heavens of intellectual existences, demolish God's throne, and blast eternal things. Sin is the opposite of good, knows no sympathy, is a fountain of malicious designs; and thus, when Jesus appears a ransom for the sinner, and by reason of the law of being, enters into sympathy with those who are the subjects of violated law, they, controlled by the principles of evil, seek to torture and destroy him, although he is the messenger of peace and good-will unto them.

"Men who are fallen, yet not immortal demons, are the occupants of the intermediate. Their souls Jesus seeks to save, and demons seek to destroy. Jesus entered their abode as their Redeemer, Apollyon approaches to destroy. With these two principles there can be no union, and therefore Jesus suffers—not by Heaven's decree, but let it be repeated, by reason of his goodness, and his mission for the sinner, and entrance into the scene of combat with death and hell."

"And shall he prevail?" inquired an angel who had listened to the address of Justice

"Yea," uttered Mercy, "he shall prevail. He is the Lion of the tribe of Judah, the bright and morning Star. He shall prevail, and shall unloose the seals." "Alleluia! he shall prevail," arose from the myriads congregated. "Thy kingdom come, thy will be done on earth as in heaven." "Even so, amen!" said Justice, and again silence prevailed.

No movement or voice disturbed the spell-bound atmosphere while Justice and Mercy paused; for it appeared that all who witnessed the scene, even the wicked on earth, and those from spheres of darkness among the regions of the dead, and those from nether abodes where evil reigns, felt the innocence of Jesus the meek sufferer. Surely it could not have been otherwise when his true character was considered. No fault could be found in him, in his life, betrayal, or when condemned to the Cross. Thus I reasoned, and thus must all conclude, when remembering that he had been betrayed—arrayed in

mock royalty before Herod—endured cruel and false
accusations of the priests. His temples had been pierced
with thorns, his back lacerated with severe scourging, and
yet he had not opened his mouth in complaint. He had
in candor replied to those interrogations, upon the answer of which it would seem his destiny depended. No
evasion of truth had stained his holy lips. Finally, in all
things he had honored his high claim to divinity, and
established his nature in righteousness.

Christ the Healer

In his life he had moved with men as a benefactor.
He had healed the sick, raised the dead, exorcised evil
spirits, restoring those who were possessed and grievously
tormented by them to quietude and happiness. He had
bound up the broken hearted; caused the mourner to
rejoice. He had forgiven transgressors, filling their hearts
with gladness and heavenly love. He had faithfully re-
proved the vile, and cleansed the temple of money
changers. And when opposed and persecuted, and even
condemned to the Cross, he had not reviled, but by his
meekness and harmony he had revealed that which could
only have been Divine.

When the cross upon which he was to be executed
was laid upon his bleeding shoulders, he had meekly
bowed under it, and borne it along, amid loud aclama-
tions and bitter taunts; thus occupying the most humiliat-
ing, as well as suffering, condition. And when fallen
beneath the Cross, exhausted in his humanity by excessive and protracted suffering, his spirit groaned, but without complaint. Then he looked upon his accusers and
tormentors with pity. Then he remembered their depraved state, and felt compassion for them. Thus the
Savior of sinners suffered, when none sympathized save
a few personal friends, whose spirits agonized with him,
but who had no means to offer aid. He bled, groaned,

fainted, and fell, but no tear stole down the hardened cheek of the cruel Jew. No soft hand touched gently his wounded temples. No words of consolation were spoken to him. Alone he endured, alone he bled, alone he struggled to bear the cross. How could those who witnessed fail to sympathize with him? or mortals refrain a tear? How fail to love one so excellent! How prevent their souls from adoring one so worthy, and the more especially since he suffered, not only innocent, but for their salvation!

He Struggles on Toward Calvary

Finally, the soldiers commanded Jesus to arise and proceed to Calvary. Obedient, he struggled beneath the cross; but his trembling limbs failed, and again he sank back in his agony. Who can depict the scene? What artist, with pencil formed of immortal colors, could so touch the sense of man, and blend the light and shadows with skill sufficient to reveal the great reality of the scene?

There was the Savior, the spotless, holy, and lovely Jesus, struggling with convulsive effort, under the scourger's lash, to raise the cross beneath which he had fallen. Blood from his bleeding body stained the ground. The severed flesh quivered from repeated strokes by the athletic scourger's hand. His swollen visage was more marred than any man's. His eye of love was concealed beneath blood and tears. His holy lips moved, prompted by his heart, which was ever full of love and pity, and they accented, "Sinner, for thee I freely suffer; for thee I endure these afflictions, yea, I endure them that thou mayest be saved."

After repeated ineffectual efforts to force Jesus to bear his cross alone, and anxious to revel in his sufferings during the final trial, orders were given to the soldiers, who compelled one Simon a Cyrenean to bear the cross. And again they proceeded.

As they advanced slowly toward Calvary, a company of females approached the dictators of the dread tragedy, and bowing before them, raised their hands, and in the most affecting manner, pleaded that Jesus should be released. No attitude could better comport with the object of their prayer. Their sorrow was inexpressible; their cause was just; their petition humble and urgent, but all of no avail. "He shall perish," said the proud priests; and again the multitude shouted, "Crucify him, crucify him. Test his power. If he be the Son of God, let him break the arm of strength that moves him toward Calvary, where his weakness, folly and blasphemy shall be revealed."

CHAPTER XXIV

JUDAS REPENTING

Before us was now displayed the Jewish sanhedrin. They were expressing many thanks for the triumph of truth over error, and of sense over fanaticism. They congratulated each other in the hope of peace that must result from the prompt and efficient action taken to put down Jesus, the impostor.

Their general appearance bespoke a proud despotic spirit rather than that of God's humble servants. There was more of jocular frivolity displayed than religion, more phariseeism than meekness, more lordship than ministry. While they were reveling in the glow of their triumphant feelings, Judas, now the picture of wretchedness, rushed into their midst and wildly exclaimed, "I have sinned in that, I have betrayed innocent blood." "What is that to us. See thou to that," replied the priests.

Judas Finds No Place for Repentance

At this cold and repulsive reply, Judas started; he had expected their sympathy and aid in his trial; and having served them, he had resorted to them for help; and their indignity offered to him upon the occasion but added sorrow to sorrow, disappointment to disappointment, remorse to remorse, and despair to wretchedness. Recovering partially from the shock produced by the unexpected reply, he at length said, "Should I not in this hour of trouble expect sympathy from those who pledged honors, blessings and friendship, to whoever would conduct them to the capture of Jesus? Did I not faithfully fulfil my engagement and give him into the hands of soldiers? Why then this cold and indifferent reply? For you I betrayed my innocent Master; for you I hailed

him in my accustomed and confident manner. Yea more,
for you I sealed my treachery with a kiss. Shall I not
now find you as faithful to your most solemn pledge?"

Then looking down as if in deep and painful thought,
he exclaimed, "When I betrayed him, he looked upon
me in love. That look I now see. I feel its power. He was
just and good. I have betrayed innocent blood." And
hastily throwing down the silver for which he had bartered Jesus, he said, "Here is the price of my Lord and
my peace for ever."

Then answered a priest, "True, that is the price; for
that we purchased thy services; why trouble us? Take
it, it is thine. We have no more need of thee. Our object
in thee is accomplished. Away, ere thou dost suffer his
fate, who goeth without the gate to receive the reward
of impious folly.

"In my complaint, thou dost acknowledge Jesus, the
outlaw, to be our king. Away, else the guard bear thee
also to Calvary."

The Depravity of the Human Heart

Then a mighty angel drew near, saying, "Behold the
procedures of men revealed in the case of Judas, the
chief priests and the rulers of the Jews. They have but
followed the native promptings of the depraved heart.
May it not then be said that the carnal mind is enmity
against God; not subject to his law, neither indeed can be.

"Are not the ways of men the reverse, and too often
designed in selfishness and clandestinely prosecuted?
Are not the tendencies of man's proceedings unrighteous?
Seeketh he not his own and not another's welfare? En-
quire of earth. Let her ages, buried in the past, relate
the history, and thus reveal the nature of the human
heart. Let the sage, the philosopher, and the poet, give
a faithful answer. Awake from their .silent repose those
who slumber in the tombs! Let lords, potentates, and

Priests, speak from their high positions, and all shall
reveal the truth that man is depraved. Let the tears and
sorows of the dependent, the servant and the slave unite,
and they shall relate the sad story of human woe, whose
source is found alone in the perversion of the heart of
man.

"Judas betrayed his Lord, and in that he bartered
justice and goodness for Mammon. His procedure has
been revealed, but his is only the great degree of that
depravity which existeth with unsanctified desires. He
sacrificed his greater good, his best friend, for applause
and gain. Doth not man often proceed on this wise? Doth
he not often barter friendship and forsake his brother,
leaving him to struggle amid accumulating sorrows; and
though earth's philosophers fain would conceal the hor-
rid picture, doth not man betray his fellow for present
gain? Whose frescoed walls and costly drapery are not
tinged with human blood? Whose luxuries may not be
traced to the sacrifice of fallen helpless brothers?

Then said another angel, who approached from an
opposite direction, "May not these truths be revealed
to the infant's understanding?"

Immediately a scene was before us, in which Earth,
with her multiform movements, was displayed.

In this scene were represented brothers betraying
brothers for gain, parents their children, husbands their
wives, friends exchanging each other as mere commod-
ities, nations in their warrings and piracy, and grievously
afflicting the poor and dependent. Multitudes of human
beings were seen suffering in lowest degradation, living
and dying without hope.

Mothers were convulsively pressing their babes for the
last time to their breasts, and imprinting upon their rosy
lips the farewell kiss, while the suckling clung with dying
hold to its mother's neck. Husbands were looking in
despair upon their maltreated wives and heart-broken

children. Poverty, oppression, pain, anguish, rapine, and murder were revealed. In the midst of these mixed multitudes were a few who were striving to unloose the fetters of those bound; to take from the scourger his cruel implements; to provide means for the sufferings of every class; to feed the hungry, clothe the naked, bind up the brokenhearted; to change war into peace; to make the battlefield a nursery for the poor and dependent; to cultivate true friendship, and enforce true religion; to enlighten the bigot; to prevent persecution, and establish with men universal liberty and harmony, founded upon justice and mercy. But their encouragement was limited. Still they failed not, but were ever engaged in deeds of benevolence.

Then a light descended, and over each of those who were engaged in the work of rescue, was a guardian angel, who, appointed of Heaven, and full of the Holy Ghost, sought to encourage them in their labors, and impress them with holy and benevolent desires. There was also revealed a light which descended from some invisible source, and which pervaded the heart of each mortal, who, in the name of the holy religion of the Cross, was struggling to lead the forlorn race.

"This," said the angel, "is Holy Inspiration. The Spirit of God, which inspireth all who are born of God, that they may labor continually for man's restoration from sin and its consequent misery, and for his final exaltation to a state of bliss."

"But," continued the angel, "no means are capable of revealing to human understanding the depth of degradation into which a heart is fallen that can be accessory to such deeds of cruelty as have just been pre-presented. And although angels with wonder behold the acts and unfaithfulness of men, so common are they with man, and so natural to his perverted being, that he not only witnesseth without regret, but may be induced to engage therein for mercenary purposes. To redeem man requires goodness beyond finite comprehension. None but God, who is Love, and who is mighty and able to save, could rescue the fallen race. Angels, while contemplating God's love bestowed upon man, exalt in thankful praise the name of our heavenly Father."

"Yea, we will adore our God for the manifestation of his love to man who is dead in trespasses and sin," answered the attending angels. "He hath laid help on one who is mighty and able to save. We will praise Him, we will praise Him evermore, amen; ever, evermore, amen." "Surely," continued the speaker, "He condescendeth to exalt the ruined orb, to harmonize the discordant race, to save the deluded spirit. He permitteth human hearts to reveal their hidden natures. In this, God is just, for heaven witnesseth, and while beholding, pitieth them. Thence angels commissioned delight to seek, as ministering spirits, the souls of men. Yea, they delight to visit earth on errands of mercy." "Angels delight to do the will of God evermore," repeated again the vast assemblage; and the guardian angels waved their hands when the scene changed.

Infants Given a Period of Rest and Relaxation

"Rest," said the chief guardian, "ye infant observers, rest, for a season mingle in the social secenes of paradisiacal enjoyment."

Then addressing a company of spirits at the right, the angel said, "Bring ye the flowers gathered upon the holy plains. Let the infant spirit be refreshed. Let the fragrance from the floral mount descend, and let joy possess each spirit. Spirit of holy quiet, pervade them with thy everlasting peace."

The entertainment introduced was wisely adapted to that quietude necessary, after the mind had been excited upon subjects so vast in magnitude, and thrilling in interest.

Then I heard a voice saying, "Who could fail to praise God for existence, for immortality, and for the bliss of paradise?" The infants caught the sound and understood the sentiment; and raising their hands, they replied, "We will adore our heavenly Father, we will ever mention with love and reverence the name of our Redeemer. We will cheerfully be led, conducted by our guardian angels. And when prepared, and our understanding properly enlarged, we will go forth as servants of goodness, whither the Lord our Redeemer shall direct.

Then each guardian moved her hand in token of a change, and all were soon in their former position.

CHAPTER XXV

CALVARY

Then a voice, full of sympathy, spake from a cloud which rested far above, saying, "Calvary revealeth her wonders. Prepare to witness the last struggle of the Redeemer, as he meets in death the destroyer."

As this voice ceased, the chief guardian raised her eyes and holy hands, saying, "O! Lord our Preserver, bestow upon us supporting aid. Preserve our minds while we may witness. Prepare us to understand. Pervade us with meekness, reverence, and holy love."

"Around this scene," continued the voice, "gather interests as lasting as immortality, as momentous as the worth of undying spirits.

"Let the sun be darkened, and the stars be veiled. Let nature pause, and heaven keep silence. Ye seraphim and ye cherubim, lay down your celestial instruments, upon which ye utter anthems most holy, while the scene transpires. Ye floral universes, droop your heads; and hang down your leaves, ye bowers. Ye waters, stand still, nor let the rippling murmur break the silence. Ye birds who warble in immortal groves be ye dumb; and pause ye breezes while the Redeemer suffers."

Then appeared Calvary beneath pale shadows. A throng was perceptible, who were apparently transfixed. In the centre were three crosses, on which, human forms were hanging. Near them were a band of soldiers, seated as if they had been engaged in gaming; but they too were fixed in an attitude, as if stunned from some unexpected cause.

Mournful murmurings were heard as though at a great distance. These murmurings seemed to still the very spirit of life in all. And a feeling of gloom, approaching utter despair, was visible upon the countenance of every spirit.

At length a low whisper passed from guardian to guardian, saying, "List! nature breathes a solemn requiem! Nature suffers. Alas! alas!" Again all was still. No sound or movement disturbed the silent gloom.

Gradually a pale light shone over Calvary, revealing more clearly the scene. And the three crosses became more visible, until the form and features of the sufferers were plainly distinguished.

"It is Jesus! Jesus suffers! Jesus expires!" burst from every spirit. A sudden shuddering seized them; and they bowed their faces, still repeating, "Jesus suffers! Jesus expires!"

While they were thus bowing, Jesus said, "Father, forgive them, for they know not what they do."

"Oh! what love, what wonderful goodness," exclaimed the humble spirits. "He prays for his crucifiers. Give us, O! thou Supreme, of that spirit evermore."

While Jesus prayed, the soldiers and the rulers derided him, saying, "He saved others; let him save himself, if he be the Christ, the chosen of God." This cold and cruel taunt caused the spirits to raise their heads, and look steadfastly upon the scene. But their sympathy and sorrow can never be revealed.

Near the Cross were bowing a few of the friends of Jesus, who were past weeping, from their excess of sorrow. Agony held them even as death holds the pale corpse. One of that little company was Mary, the mother of Jesus, who had ever lingered near him during his sufferings, but who appeared conscious of the certainty of his trial. She suffered with him. As a holy mother she suffered, but could not save.

Jesus turning his eye upon the group, said to Mary, "Woman, behold thy son." Then addressing the beloved disciple, he said, "Behold thy mother." And thus in his agony he displayed his humanity, and invited the disciple to support Mary who was sinking beneath her weight of grief.

The disciple then supported Mary, who leaned upon him as she looked upon her Son in his last trial.

Conversion of the Thief on the Cross

Then one of the malefactors who was crucified with Jesus, railed on him, saying, "If thou be Christ, save thyself and us." To this the Lord made no reply, but looked in pity upon him. The other malefactor rebuked his fellow, saying, "We receive the due reward of our deeds, but this man hath done nothing amiss." Then in a devout manner said to Jesus, "Those who have let thee here exult in their folly. They vainly suppose thee conquered and slain; but I feel from thee an influence superior to man. Thou art from everlasting to everlasting. Mystery hangeth about thee, O Lord! I know that in thee exist the fountains of life. Thou livest evermore. Wilt thou, O Lord, remember me when thou comest into thy kingdom?" Then the Lord looked upon him, and love from his spirit overshadowed and pervaded the suppliant. The Holy Spirit wrought in his heart that change necessary to his union with the enduring principles of divine life and love. And in answer to his prayer, Jesus said, "Inasmuch as thou hast from thy heart sought help, thy prayer is answered. Verily I say unto thee, this day shalt thou be with me in paradise." This reply was like life given to the dead; and the malefactor, although in the agonies of death, manifested that emotion which bespoke a soul forgiven, a spirit made free. His was a reprieve, not from the execution of the sentence of an earthly tribunal, but Heaven's pardon—a release from the power of sin and death. He feared no more. All heaven, through Jesus, had been secured in the last and trying moment. His physical sufferings appeared to operate as holy enchantment to charm the body to rest, while the soul shone forth amid the darkness, and hovered over the death-gulf ready for its happy flight—its exit from death to life, from mortality to the possession of eternal realities. While this scene was transpiring, the mockers around the cross had not noticed the Divinity of Jesus manifested in the forgiveness of sin. But the angels and infants beheld with wonder and gratitude the goodness displayed in that trying moment. And so deep was the impression, that ever after, when referring to the crucifixion, the infants would name the thief, speak of his prayer, and the propitious answer of the Redeemer,—that answer by which all heaven was given to the dying sinner.

CHAPTER XXVI

DEATH OF THE SAVIOR

Darkness now began to fold more closely its mantle around the scene. No sun, or moon, or stars were visible. Night in heavy gloom veiled the earth.

At length Jesus said, "I thirst;" whereupon one filled a sponge with vinegar, and put it upon hyssop, and touched his parched lips. This was too much for the infants; and at the sight, they drooped as if immortality had failed; their guardians took them in their arms and supported them.

Death Challenges the Savior

While witnessing the scene, which only revealed cruelty added to cruelty, a form, terrible in appearance, approached Jesus, around whose ghostly visage, like satellites, revolved unnumbered lesser creatures the image of himself. "Thou shalt triumph, thou triumphant king," was written in broad capitals upon the sphere that encompassed him. His appearance was like one sure of victory when engaging in the final conflict—a conflict upon the issue of which depended the interests of ages. With a hoarse, sepulchral voice, a voice of terror, and in a manner characteristic of a never-failing conqueror, he addressed Jesus, who hung upon the cross, saying, "I arise and meet thee in this thy day of folly. Thou art chained. Thou art a victim. Angels, saints, and men have shouted thy triumph over death. Death is my name. Thou hast engaged to reverse that law by which I exist—that law which feeds the hungry tombs with the bodies of infants, youths, and hoary age; that law which has moved in might, and none can hinder; that law which this day grapples with thee, and thou too shalt perish. Lo, I come to seize this vase, and dash it against the marble rock of dissolution." Then reaching forth his hand, he seized the body of Jesus, whose sensitive nerves quivered from the touch of his cold contracting fingers.

Then Jesus cried, "Eloi, eloi, lama sabachthani. My God, my God, why hast thou forsaken me." Upon which a voice said from above, "He treadeth the wine-press alone."

"Nevertheless," answered another voice, "he suffereth, the just for the unjust." "Then," shouted Death, "I have gotten the victory. He who was in the beginning with God, entereth the destructive elements where violated law breaketh in pieces the violator. He entereth that he may rescue, and shall also perish. He faileth. Let hades arise and behold my triumph; and ye angelic hosts who came to witness, behold and wonder while Jesus struggles in my right hand. Ye have sung through all heaven that he should vanquish death. Yea, see how he struggles while I hold him with my might. I alone grasp this 'God-man,' and leap with him amid the tombs. Ah ha! ah ha! chant ye his victory! Chant rather his defeat. I hold the conqueror. Give back ye heavens, ere I ascend from sphere to sphere, and shake the eternal throne, and make of celestial worlds a cemetery for the dead." Then with wild exultant glare, he met the Savior's face, and with menacing reproach said, "How vain for thee to seek this issue? Have I not slain unnumbered legions? And thinkest thou to escape? Nay, Jesus, thou 'God-man,' I sacrifice thee, my last foe."

Around this scene had again congregated the hosts of vile spirits—Apollyon leading in his triumph—waving in the infernal breezes their black banners, upon which appeared the figures of Apollyon, the embodiment of evil, and Death the fell destroyer, embracing each other over the image of the cross and bleeding sacrifice. Then followed bold blasphemies, boisterous shouting, and wild demoniac laughter. The messengers of evil moved like waves of thick and black waters to and fro; while their hellish jubilee burst forth as from a compressed sea of madness and fiendish delight.

They moved around Jesus, shouting "Ah ha! ah ha!" while Death was addressing him, and their triumph appeared sure.

The infants, upon beholding this scene, inquired, "Shall they triumph, and Jesus die?"

"If Jesus perish," answered an angel, " the heavens fail. He holdeth the universe in his right hand."

"But," said Apollyon in distant reply, "he faileth in this decisive hour. Strike your death song, ye congregated millions! for, lo! Jesus the boasted Son of God is at last subdued. Death prevaileth!"

Then the divinity of Jesus said, "No man taketh my life. I lay it down of myself. Ye who seek me, employ men in the external world as agents of slaughter and execution; but they have no power over me save what is given them. Lo! I come through death's portals to bind thee, thou destroyer; and from thy power, rescue my people—those whom I redeem.

"That I may prevail, I meet thee in thy dominions. Lo, I come! Thou art involved in thine own design. I meet thee, not in vengeance, but to open the tomb and set the captives free; to open the prison-door of those bound and imprisoned; to bind thee and destroy thy power. I have descended amid dissolving elements: humanity being the chariot in which I enter the dark dominions where mortality faileth. Thou art conquered. The law of life and harmony shall entwine thy form, and establish the boundaries of thy dominions. And thus shalt thou await that day when death and hell shall be cast into the bottomless abyss, and they shall no more afflict my people."

Death Bound by the Redeemer

Thus saying, he bound Death with a chain of light.

Then raising his eyes toward Justice, who witnessed from the cloud, he said, "Behold! the Spirit of Life prevaileth over death." And addressing the roaring tempest of dissolving nature which gathered its mighty maelstrom around him, and broke in fearful whirlpools upon him, he said, "Stay, thou angry flood! Roll back your waters ye death currents! Unloose thy grasp thou boasting conqueror, thou prince of terrors! Lo! I come to rescue the fallen orb, ere it plunge into the bottomless abyss." Then raising his right hand of divine strength, while standing in the mighty cataract of dissolving nature, he touched an orb, which, in its wandering revolutions, had neared, and by attraction from the abyss, hung upon the brink ready to plunge, with its swarming and distracted millions of inhabitants, amid the surging billows that drive madly down the gulf of death. While thus holding the suspended orb, he said, "Stay thou tempest, terrible in might! Although thy waves fearfully gather around the fallen world; although thy current draws with immensity of strength; although thou hast forced that Earth along the death surges of ages, be thou still! Earth, reverse thy movement. Arise! the day of thy salvation dawneth. Ye mighty winds of heaven, fan into life the expiring orb. Ye pure waters, ever flowing from life's ceaseless fountains, let your cooling tides move over her parched and barren soil. And ye angels who minister in love, gather quickly around the discordant race, administer life's cordials, and with truth, antidote the evil of false and perverted hearts. Bar ye the gateway to immortal slumbers, that forlorn man may not enter there. And thou Death," he continued, "although thou dost boast thy millions slain, upon thee I fix my seal; thou art bound, and thy days are numbered. Hades, thy kingdom of mortality, the trophy of victorious ages, shall fail. And thou, at the time appointed, having no more kingdoms to demolish, shalt die."

Then addressing Apollyon, he said, "Thou foe of equity, harmony, peace, and heaven, depart quickly to regions whence thou art. Lead thy forces deathward, for at the time appointed, thou too, shalt feel restraining power. Lo! I come to rescue my people."

Jesus then moved his hand, and Apollyon with his legions departed, and a dark cloud which accompanied, concealed them from our view.

The Lord then said, "Father, into thy hands I commit my spirit;" and with a loud voice, cried, "It is finished;" and then holding Death subject to his will, descended to the spirits in prison.

The Tomb

The scene of the crucifixion had scarcely passed, when the land of Canaan appeared, manifesting that inactivity consequent upon over-excitement, occasioned by the agitation of some momentous question of national policy.

A soft light gently descended, revealing a solitary tomb, around which were stationed armed guards. To that tomb was entrusted the body of Jesus. An angel standing near, touched the tomb with a sceptre he held in his right hand, and it became to us transparent, revealing the body in its quiet rest.

It calmly reposed in the lone sepulchre, shrouded in clean linen unstained by blood. The still and noiseless atmosphere, undisturbed by the clamor of the shouting rabble, and the sweet sleep of that body, as now presented in its unmolested home, conspired to give that relief which could not fail to soothe the minds of those who had been overwhelmed by the revolting scenes of cruelty and slaughter, which had been displayed during that awful period in which the Lord suffered.

"How calm, how composed is now the body of Jesus!"

said the chief guardian, while we were enjoying rest of spirits as we looked upon it.

"Yea, Jesus resteth," answered a voice, and Mercy appeared above the tomb. "Yea, he resteth, He maketh the tomb his bed. With his people he slumbereth in the grave. He sanctified the sepulchre of his saints. But he sleepeth to awake again. He also shall awaken all who sleep in death."

Then one of the celestial choirs descended and chanted over the tomb where Jesus lay.

"Peace and quiet slumber, holy rest, fold gently in thy gracious arms the body of the Lord, which no more endureth pain forever. Holy angels, guard the sacred tomb. Let no intruder pass the portals of this temple where the body of the Redeemer resteth. Stay the dissolving elements, that they change it not. Let it not see corruption. Let not worms feed upon it. It hath been sanctified through suffering."

Then in a loud acclaim, another company of angels chanted, "It shall arise again. It shall ascend to the highest heaven. It shall be the attractive centre around which saints shall gather. It shall attract unto itself, in the realms of immortality, the sanctified dust, the renovated bodies of the saints."

Again, chanted the choir above, "Let the heavens resume their lyres, and strike their highest notes to lofty anthems. Jesus shall awake and ascend in clouds of glory. Universes shall join the song of his ascension. Echo, ye everlasting hills, echo ye his name in triumphant song."

It was joy beyond measure to see the body of Jesus rest. It was sacred quiet. It was fulness of harmony to listen to the soft anthems of the angel band that watched the tomb. Surely it may be said that Jesus sanctified the grave. I can never reflect upon that scene without a desire that my poor body should rest there also. I wish to lay it down in the tomb. The grave no longer wears a gloom.

To me it is the most sacred place of all on earth. There Jesus my Redeemer slumbered. There his body rested. There it was free from pain. Only let me be worthy, and cheerfully, at the time appointed, will I step into the grave, and lay my body down to rest, where, in peace, it shall await the morning of the resurrection.

CHAPTER XXVII

THE RESURRECTION AND ASCENSION

"Behold and wonder, ye inhabitants of paradise," said a mighty angel as he descended and stood upon the tomb. "Yea, behold, as the Son of Man cometh from the abode of desolation, lo! he cometh a conqueror from the regions of the dead."

While he yet spake, Jesus, even the Incarnate Spirit, the Spirit of Redemption, appeared walking among the tombs. And as he looked over them, he said, "Here sleep the bodies of my people. Long and dreary hath been the night of your slumbers, and cold the couch on which ye have reposed. Massive walls, enclosing this vast arena, have guarded and confined you while ye have slept. Precious dust thou art, since thou hast been the dwelling of spirits I redeem. Thou shalt arise. This darkness which hath so long shrouded thy abode in night, adding gloom to gloom, shall be dispersed by the light of life. Lo, I come to illumine this dark and solitary vault, this charnel-house of the dead,—to determine the limits of death and the grave, and to open a door of escape. Sleep on, ye sacred relics. Dust of my people. Sleep on until thou art animated by the quickening, purifying, and exalting principle of eternal law. Sleep on until life from on high shall redeem and spiritualize these properties of nature; and prepare the atoms of the sphere of rudimental life for the immortal and incorruptible habitations of the spirit in its spiritual existence. Sleep on until that day, when thou art called from this silent slumber to spheres of life. The tomb shall be illumined. Henceforth the totality of its darkness shall be no more."

The Resurrection of the Righteous Dead

Then lifting his eyes, he said, "Watchman from the

everlasting hills, descend and enter thou this abode. Keep guard until the morning of the Resurrection, when I will bid thee arise with these ashes, which, quickened into life, refined, purified, and reorganized, shall become the outer garment of my redeemed people. That day in divine certainty surely cometh." The one, mighty in strength, whose garment reflected ten thousand interwoven crosses, entered the arena, from the mount of light, and addressing Jesus, said, "Lo! I come to do thy will, O God."

The Lord then replied, "Guard thou this sepulchre where mortality slumbereth;" and placing in his right hand a sceptre, upon whose burnished shaft, was engraven the image of the cross; and also in hieroglyphics, the solemn events of the trial and crucifixion, Jesus said, "With this sceptre thou shalt defend and control these dominions until Heaven calleth for thee." The watchman answered, "Be thou my help; thy will be done evermore."

Resurrection of Christ

The Divine Spirit then approached a lone tomb, even that which angels watched, and in which reposed the body of Jesus; and with a voice that indicated supreme power, said, "Let Life descend upon this inanimate form. Let the Quickening Spirit pervade and quicken this body. Let every function, tissue, and property thereof, be transformed into life, and thus immortalized: let this body arise."

Then light from the Divine Spirit encompassed the body, and a sudden shaking seized the walls and foundation of the tombs.

And the body of Jesus arose. Whereupon a mighty angel said, with a loud voice, "Jesus prevaileth; he ariseth triumphant. Death hath no power over him; he breaketh the strong bands thereof; he liveth evermore. Raise your anthems high all ye who dwell in worlds of light: Jesus reigns. "Hallelujah! amen! Jesus reigns!" answered the

156 Scenes Beyond the Grave

innumerable companies of angels, who had witnessed the reanimation and resurrection of the body. "But although ye shout him victorious, he remaineth with the dead," said Justice, who was still observing the scene.

Then Jesus approached the massive gate, which shut the passage from the tomb, and reaching forth his hand, touched its mighty bars, and lo! they crumbled to dust. He then said, "Be unbarred thou mighty gate—Lo! thy keeper, even Death, hath no more power over thee. His limits are determined. Yea, even although, through the violation of the law of life, man faileth; and as Adam perished even so the outer man wasteth away and dieth; yet in Jesus, by the law of life revealed through the Incarnate Spirit, man shall be restored; he shall live again.

"The grave shall not have everlasting dominion over the ashes of the dead, nor exist as a perpetual vale of darkness between earth and the regions occupied by those spirits departed from the outer world."

Then said Jesus, "Open ye massive gate; and ye winds bear it away that it may return no more forever."

The gate then disappeared, and Jesus moved his right hand over the silent slumberers, saying, "This dust shall awake; it shall be quickened and prepared for the habitation of disembodied spirits."

"How shall these awake? How shall the grave give up their dead?" enquired a voice, and lo! Justice appeared above the gateway.

Then Jesus arose from the tomb, holding in his hand the keys of the dark dominions.

And a voice spake from a cloud which rested above the scene, saying, "This is my beloved Son; the hope of Israel; the bright and morning star. Peace be unto the world."

The cloud then descended, and as it approached Jesus, Mercy moved therefrom, and addressing Justice, said,

"This is the offering I bring, and this is the trophy of his victory, even the body of Jesus now raised from the tomb and made immortal. Dost thou, O Justice, accept the offering?" Justice replied, "The offering is accepted since divine power immortalized the properties of the outer man giving life to that from which life had departed.

Then said Mercy, "The offering ariseth in perfection, animate with divine life, and shall henceforth be glorified. In Jesus, the Divine Spirit came to seek and save perverted man, even as a faithful shepherd seeketh the lost sheep strayed from the fold; and henceforth salvation shall be preached to the forlorn race; and hope like a star of superior light shall guide the wanderer to the port of peace. Jesus controlleth the fury of discordant elements, henceforth they shall not drive the humble mariner to the regions of eternal night. At the gateway of death, remaineth the mighty watchman, who, by divine appointment, guardeth the cold sepulcher. Heaven hath determined that death shall give up her dead in the last day; that day appointed, when God shall make up his jewels; and shall spare all who love and obey him, even as a man spareth his own son that serveth him."

Justice Acknowledges the Ransom

Then Justice, addressing Jesus, said, "Thou art from everlasting to everlasting, King of kings and Lord of lords. Thou hast the keys of death. Heaven accepts the offering and acknowledges the victory. Thy mission, trial, and conquest, is inscribed upon the Throne of eternal recollection. Henceforth the Cross is engraven upon, and inwrought throughout all things in the kingdom of righteousness—to be kept in everlasting remembrance.

"Lo! I come to thee, thou Lamb slain for sinners; yea, thou upon whose shoulders resteth the government of peace. I embrace thee. Thou art God." Thus saying, Justice embraced Jesus, and Mercy said, "Shall the sinner, even he who lieth in his fallen condition, be rescued? Shall he find favor?" Justice replied, "God in Christ reconcileth the world to himself, and through his mediation, Heaven shall be just in the justification of all who come to God through Him. If the sinner forsake the evil of his way, and the unrighteous man his thoughts, and return unto the Lord, he shall obtain favor. He who seeketh life, shall in Jesus enjoy the blessings of everlasting righteousness unto peace. Then Mercy raising her hands and eyes to heaven, said, 'Now is salvation complete. Henceforth, thy glory, O God! shineth upon the fallen orb. And thy name shall be adored by all who have immortality, because thou hast provided means for the salvation of man.' "

Thus saying, Mercy also embraced Jesus, and a cloud of light encompassed them, whereupon Justice and Mercy so blended in the sphere of the Lord as to lose identy, and they were thereafter only revealed as in the person of Jesus, who, with that cloud amid the hallelujahs of legions, arose from the tomb.

Believers Given the Ministry of Deliverance

Before us now appeared the afflicted disciples, who, having met in a mountain by special appointment of their Lord, were communing with each other relative to the resurrection. Suddenly a light shone upon them, and Jesus appeared in their midst, and said, "Fear not; all power is given unto me in heaven and on earth. Go ye, therefore, and preach the Gospel unto all nations; baptizing them in the name of the Father, and of the Son, and of the Holy Ghost; teaching them to observe all things whatsoever I command you: and, lo, I am with you alway, even unto the end of the world. Ye shall be persecuted of men for my name's sake: but I have overcome; and ye shall also overcome if ye trust my word. *These signs shall follow those that believe. In my name they shall cast out devils; they shall speak with new tongues; they shall take up serpents; and if they drink any deadly thing, it shall not hurt them; they shall lay their hands on the sick, and they shall recover. But tarry ye in the city of Jerusalem until endued with power from on high."*

The Ascension

Then he lifted up his hands and blessed them. While blessing them he arose, and a cloud received him out of their sight.

Then the unnumbered millions, who filled the heavens, with strong hands swept the chords of their stringed instruments, and, with loud voices, said, "We give thee thanks, O Lord God Almighty, which was, and is, and is to come; because thou hast taken to thee thy great power, and hast conquered. We praise thee, O Lord, who art King of kings, and Lord of lords; the Alpha and Omega, the Beginning and the End, the First and the Last."

During the Ascension, the disciples had steadfastly looked up into heaven, whither had gone their arisen and ascended Lord. But as the cloud which received him from their sight finally disappeared, they worshiped; and afterwards, in silence arose and departed for Jerusalem.

Chapter XXVIII

THE RESCUE

The former scenes having passed, we heard an angel, with a loud voice, proclaim, "Now salvation appeareth. Hope ye inhabitants of earth; yea, rejoice; for the Lion of the tribe of Judah hath prevailed to open the book, and unloose the seven seals thereof. Let salvation, the year of jubilee, be proclaimed afar. Go forth, ye messengers; declare the love of God as made manifest in the rescue of the bewildered race. Yea, let the heavens echo the glad news; for God so loved the world that he gave his only-begotten Son; that whosoever believeth in him should not perish, but have everlasting life."

As the angel spake, we heard a voice of lamentation, saying, "O wretched man that I am! who shall deliver me from the body of this death?"

From the direction of the voice arose a cloud, displaying frightful tempests. A little beyond that cloud arose lofty mountains, from whose very side appeared to issue fire and smoke in all the terrors of warring elements.

Again the voice of bitter wailing, "Must we perish!"

The Scene of the Forlorn Man

The dark cloud which overhung the scene, parting, we beheld, by the aid of a pale light, the forlorn man and his friends,—the same displayed in a former scene. By them stood a man clad in simple apparel. He was holding in his hand a book, from which he read, "Come unto me, all ye that labor and are heavy laden, and I will give you rest." As he read, the afflicted man looked up, and although somewhat disturbed by his presence, said, "To whom may I go? In whom shall I have hope?"

"In Jesus, who is the Savior of men," answered the messenger.

"But I am polluted from the sole of the foot to the crown of the head," continued the fallen man.

Then the messenger read from the book again, "Though thy sins be as scarlet, they shall be as white as snow; though they be as crimson, they shall be as wool."

The sufferer replied, "I have sinned against heaven."

Again the messenger read, "Let the wicked forsake his way, and the unrighteous man his thoughts; and let him return unto the Lord, and he will have mercy upon him; and to our God, for he will abundantly pardon." Then said he, "It is also written, The whole need not a physician, but they that are sick. If thou seekest to enter into life with all thy heart thou mayest. Look up," he continued, as he raised his hand, and immediately a light shone from above, revealing to the inward sense of the sufferer, the Redeemer as extended upon the cross; and he heard a voice saying, "No man cometh unto the Father but by me. I am the Way, the Truth, and the Life. He that believeth on me, though he were dead, yet shall he live; and whosoever liveth and believeth on me, shall never die. Believest thou this?"

The Sinner Saved and Healed

The sufferer replied, "Lord, I believe; help thou mine unbelief;" and raising his hands he prayed, "God be merciful to me a sinner." And a light descended, resting upon him; and the Spirit of God pervading his soul, spake to his spirit, *"Thy sins are forgiven thee; thy guilt removed; thy wounds are healed;* the Spirit quickeneth thee, bidding thee arise, for salvation hath come unto thee."

Then the redeemed man arose, and rejoicing worshiped; and the light that shone upon him revealed his inner being, upon which was impressed the image of the Cross; and upon his heart was written the law of heaven.

Again the messenger, who still stood near him, read, "Blessed are the pure in heart; for they shall see God."

Then addressing him, said, "Quickened by the Spirit, thou
hast passed from death unto life; and art restored to
harmony, and clothed with the garments of salvation.
Go forth, saith the Spirit, proclaim the Grace of God, by
which thou hast been redeemed. The harvest is truly
great, but the laborers are few. Go preach the Gospel;
seek the lost. Freely thou hast received, freely give. This
is the spirit of the Gospel of the Lord our Redeemer. Be
faithful to the grace given thee. Watch, that when thy
Lord cometh and calleth for thee, thou mayest give account of thy stewardship." Then he read again, "Lo! I
am with thee, to bless and strengthen thee. For every trial
my grace shall be sufficient."

Thanksgiving of the Redeemed Man

The redeemed man then raised his eyes to heaven,
and prayed, "Be thou, O God, my help. I can do all things
if Jesus Christ strengthen me;" and, as a servant of the
Cross, an ambassador of Jesus, he entered the cloud, which
made dark and gloomy the plain at the foot of the mountain. And as he departed, we heard him say, "O Lord,
truly I am thy servant: thou hast loosed my bonds. What
shall I render unto the Lord for all his benefits to me? I
will offer the sacrifice of thanksgiving, and call upon the
name of the Lord. I will pay my vows unto the Lord now
in the presence of all his people. Search me, then, O God,
by thy Spirit, and try me, and see if there be any evil way
in me; and lead me in the way everlasting. O praise the
Lord, all ye nations: praise him, all ye people; for his
merciful kindness is great toward men. The truth of the
Lord endureth for ever. Praise ye the Lord."

Then an innumerable company of redeemed spirits
drew near, and, led by Mary the mother of Jesus, chanted
with loud voices, "We will praise thee, O Lord God Almighty, which was, and is, and is to come, for thy wondrous works with the children of men! Just and true are

thy ways, thou Prince and Author of salvation! Thou
hast redeemed us! When we were not mindful of thee,
thy Spirit sought us! Worthy is the Lamb! Wondrous are
thy works, O thou who dwellest above the cherubim;
whose throne is the eternity of cause; whose dominion
is over all! Praise, glory, and dominion be unto thee,
throughout everlasting ages! Amen!

Finally, an angel addressing me, said, "These infants,
having been prepared, will ascend to a more exalted plane
—a realm where, blessed with superior advantages, and
surrounded with still brighter glories, they shall arise
from one degree of attainment to another, and shall bathe
in crystal waters ever flowing. And they shall glide in
crystaline barges over the smooth and transparent floods
of never-failing rivers, and shall gather fruit from the
groves and flowering vines that ever adorn the banks
of those placid waters.

"The glory of that sphere descends; and spirits, whose
duty it is to lead these infants upward, receive them from
their former guardians. Let us arise."

CHAPTER XXIX

MARIETTA'S RETURN TO EARTH

The period at length drew near when I was to return to the world; and the infants, their attending angels, and those who had been employed in the various scenes, were congregated together. They sung a soft and melodious hymn, during which they fixed their attention upon me. I felt more than ever their love, and the value of heaven and heavenly associations. At length the spirit who had kissed the Cross approached me, leading the two children, as on a former occasion, and addressing me, said, "Marietta, for a season thou art to leave us. We love and deeply sympathize with thee. Thou art beloved of all; but it is our Redeemer's pleasure, and we cheerfully submit. Marietta, we joy in the precious promise of thy return at a time appointed."

"Yea, in this we rejoice," said the multitude.

"We rejoice also," continued the spirit, "because thou hast been permitted to visit, in spirit, these realms, and to behold some of the beauties, and to realize the harmony and divine order of paradisiacal abodes and of angelic worship. Yea more, we praise our heavenly Father, because thou hast been permitted to witness the mode by which infants are instructed in the great truths of man's perverted nature, and also the means provided for his redemption. Moreover, it fills us with delight to know that thou hast not only been permitted to behold, but thou hast been received and blessed by the Redeemer, in whom we have life, and through whom we obtain heaven. We will give thee our spirit of love, and, as one, we will embrace thee, and patiently wait the happy period when we shall hail thee at the gate of the Holy City upon thy return."

The Farewell

Then all arose and formed themselves into circles around me, and encompassed me as in a dome of spirits; and the spirit who had addressed me pressed me to her heart, when I felt their influences as the embrace of one. Present reflections upon that scene fill my soul with ecstasy, and to attempt its description is in vain. After this manifestation of love, the spirit led the two children to me, and they entwined their holy arms around my neck, and pressed kiss after kiss upon my lips, saying, "Marietta, when thou art again with those in the outer world who love us, and who have mourned our loss, tell them we are happy; that we have no sorrow; we are ever with our guardians; that we love all, and Jesus our Redeemer above all. Tell them we shall wait with patience their arrival here. We love thee, Marietta, and will meet thee again." They once more embraced me, and withdrew; and the spirit who led them to me said, "Marietta, trust thy Redeemer evermore. Relate on earth the story of Redemption. Do well thy work of love."

The Lord Gives Marietta a Charge

Then from a cloud Jesus descended, and placing his hand upon my head, addressed me, saying, "Child, for a wise purpose thou art to return. Be faithful to thy charge. Relate, as thou art able, what thou hast seen and heard. Fulfill thy mission, and, at the time appointed, angels shall meet thee at the gate of death, and bear thee to mansions in the kingdom of peace. Be not sad; my grace shall sustain thee. In thy sufferings thou shalt be supported." Then an angel gave him a golden goblet, and he placed it to my lips. As I drank I was filled with new life and fortitude to endure the separation, and I bowed and worshiped him; and he with his right hand raised me up, saying, "Child of sorrow from a world of gloom, thou art redeemed, thou art blessed for evermore. Be faithful, and when thy course on earth is ended, thou shalt enter into the joy of thy Lord." Then placing in my hand an olive branch, he said, "Bear this to earth, as thou hast been instructed." Again he laid his hand upon my head, and light and love filled my spirit.

Departure to Earth

The time had come for my departure. I looked around upon the scenes of that lovely city and upon its happy inhabitants. I offered myself in thanksgiving to God for the blessings of immortality, and, above all, for the gift of grace in Jesus, who is the Redeemer; and before the multitudes I lifted to my Lord my hands and a voice in prayer for support in that hour, that I might be kept in his love who had blessed me. Then I was borne in the arms of angels to the gateway of the temple, where I first met the Lord; and from thence—while angels chanted praise to God and to the Lamb—with my former guide I descended to earth; and entering this room where my body lay I soon awoke.

Patiently I wait the hour which I know is determined, when I shall go hence and enjoy the fruition of those realms of bliss, where my spirit obtained its assurance of joys to come. I will praise my heavenly Father for my hope in Jesus, which is worth ten thousand worlds to me. And when I arrive in Paradise, free from mortality, I will praise him with an undivided and pure heart, and with holy lips. There I will, in loud anthems, exalt the name of my Redeemer while eternity endures.

THE END

Christ For The Nations
M a g a z i n e

FREE
One Year
Subscription

Christ For The Nations' monthly magazine includes motivational articles, an informative *World Prayer & Share Letter*, a missions project, updates regarding CFN's annointed conferences - and news about what's happening at CFN's interdenominational Bible institute, which is training world changers for the 21st century.
Please send request to:

Christ For The Nations ● P.O. Box 769000
Dallas, TX 75376-9000 ● (214) 376-1711
www.cfni.org

Please include your name, address, phone, e-mail and date of birth.

* overseas subscriptions, please pay $10.00

Christ For The Nations
International Missions

Literature Program

International Bible Schools

Support to Orphans

Native Church Program

Humanitarian Aid & World Relief

CHRIST FOR THE NATIONS
P.O. Box 769000 • Dallas, TX 75376-9000
1-800-933-2364 • www.cfni.org